# STEALING GLIMPSES

# STEALING GLIMPSES

OF POETRY,
POETS, AND THINGS
IN BETWEEN

ESSAYS BY
Molly McQuade

Sarabande Books
LOUISVILLE, KENTUCKY

FIRST EDITION

Managing Editor
Sarabande Books, Inc.
2234 Dundee Road, Suite 200
Louisville, KY 40205

LIBRARY OF CONGRESS CATALOGING-IN-PUBLICATION DATA

McQuade, Molly.
Stealing glimpses : of poetry, poets, and things in between / by
Molly McQuade.
       p.      cm.
ISBN 1-889330-25-6 (cloth : alk. paper). — ISBN 1-889330-26-4 (pbk. :
alk. paper)
1. American poetry—20th century—History and criticism.
I. Title.
PS323.5.M4    1999
810.9'005—dc21                                          98-26855
                                                             CIP

Jacket photograph of the Gotham Book Mart by Lina Palotta. Used by kind permission of the photographer.

Cover and text design by Charles Casey Martin.

Manufactured in the United States of America.
This book is printed on acid-free paper.

Sarabande Books is a nonprofit literary organization.

Publication of this book was made possible, in part, by a grant from the National Endowment for the Arts.

# ACKNOWLEDGMENTS

☒

Emily Dickinson's poems #1563, 1695, 1365, 1429, 1596, 258, 1261 reprinted by permission of the publishers and Trustees of Amherst College from *The Poems of Emily Dickinson*, Thomas H. Johnson, ed., Cambridge, Massachusetts: The Belknap Press of Harvard University Press. Copyright © 1951, 1955, 1979, 1983 by the President and Fellows of Harvard College.

"Delta" from *Time's Power: Poems 1985–1988* by Adrienne Rich. Copyright © 1989 by Adrienne Rich. Reprinted by permission of the author and W. W. Norton & Company, Inc.

"Snapshots of a Daughter-in-Law" from *Collected Early Poems: 1950–1970* by Adrienne Rich. Copyright © 1963, 1967, 1993 by Adrienne Rich. Reprinted by permission of the author and W. W. Norton & Company, Inc.

"Paradise" from *The Book of Gods and Devils*. Copyright © 1990 by Charles Simic. Reprinted by permission of Harcourt Brace & Company.

"Saint Francis and the Sow" from *Mortal Acts, Mortal Words* by Galway Kinnell. Copyright © 1980 by Galway Kinnell. Reprinted by permission of Houghton Mifflin Company. All rights reserved.

The author would like to thank the Pew Charitable Trusts, the New York Foundation for the Arts, the MacDowell Colony, the Ucross Foundation, the Squaw Valley Community of Writers, and the Wesleyan Writers Conference for assistance and support in the writing of these essays.

# CONTENTS

⩔

# STEALING GLIMPSES

# A Word Predator

LATELY, I'VE BEEN TAKING dream dictation from E. B. White. He tells me sinuously in my sleep how to write and what to think. He urges me to be more serious, yet light on my feet—virtuous, like a verb that spins away. White's style, a passion while he lived, is assertively nonchalant. His wisdom is impossible to retrieve, word for word, the morning after. Still, I wake up knowing that I have been instructed in loomingly small points of how to fashion words into something good enough, if not better. The form taken by the words—poetry or prose—seems unimportant. The lesson offered concerns precision, composition, and boldness. I hardly dare learn it well enough to repeat it.

This tale must sound freakish. Yet the experience is dauntingly actual. I can't quarrel with it. If anything, I wish that these dreams were *more* fanciful. For it's terrifying to submit, against your will, to a teacher who's a stylist. The sensation of learning can break you. You may have to decide to give up what you knew, losing your cynicism, your common sense, and the skill you taught yourself when certain that the world had mainly bad things to teach you. It all makes you feel incontinent and larval. Since you are in New York, there are times when you feel still worse, like a pulp on the street about to be kicked or killed by a large seeing-eye dog.

I would have accepted a nocturnal tutorial more readily from Emily Dickinson or Allen Ginsberg, difficult as that, too, might have been. They're poets; I would have listened. Unlike them, White is not regarded as one, although from time to time he wrote and published verse. "To me," he remarked, "poetry is what is memorable, and a poet is a fellow or girl who lets drop a line that gets remembered in the morning. Poetry turns up in unexpected places, in unguarded moments." It turns up even in the manuscripts of blithely self-abasing poet-journalists. In a poem called "H. L. Mencken Meets a Poet in the West Side Y.M.C.A.," White wrote, perhaps in part about himself, "Poetry is the sleepy weed/The dumb, the sick, and the dizzy need." He confessed in the preface to his collected verse: "Having lived happily all my life as a non-poet who occasionally breaks into song, I have no wish at this late hour to change either my status or my habits even if I were capable of doing so, and I clearly am not. The life of a non-poet is an agreeable one: he feels no obligation to mingle with other writers of verse to exchange sensitivities, no compulsion to visit the 'Y' to read from his own works, no need to travel the wine-and-cheese circuit, where the word 'poet' carries the aroma of magic and ladies creep up from behind carrying ballpoint pens and sprigs of asphodel."

In the 1930s, '40s, and '50s, White instead wrote essays for *The New Yorker*; his cool, plain-mannered chic and wit are closely linked with that magazine's. And he is well known as the author of two novels for children, *Charlotte's Web* and *Stuart Little*. But whatever his disclaimers, I now believe that White was essentially a poet, and was also a frustrated poet. If he hadn't been both at once, he wouldn't have mattered as a writer. And he wouldn't matter to me.

Because I didn't always accept White naturally as a writerly influence, I have had to listen harder to him now. There has been a fight. (The fight continues.) He talks to me when, semiconscious, I can't answer back, in an unevenly matched set-to over writers' issues: diction, concision, accuracy, imagination, and other midnight fantasies.

So now I am supposed to explain and justify this ghostly, scampish influence.

The likely source of his frustration: his merit as a journalist would have seemed to rule out poetic accomplishment, even footloose dallying with the notion. And at times, journalism did rule this out for him. But not often enough to deny poetry's potential place in a paragraph. Somehow, he fit poetry in.

Frustration actually consolidated his strength. Frustration honed and qualified his fascination with a word, or with a few words. The few did battle with the many. The goal was to choose. We all do choose, yet may forget the stakes. He reminds me what they are. Subtleties like these have been a part of my initiation and instruction.

Owing to my own frustration with White's nightly partnership, I have been spending the days rereading him, trying to fathom him as a poet. Maybe because expository prose rarely radiates the sheen of poetic choice—of these several words, and *not* those—I am irrationally smitten, finding in White's typical modesty the élan or bravado of a word predator.

The predator, even if frustrated, is impelled by nerve and gaiety, like a stray cat at large in an old-fashioned bookshop. He specializes in anachronistic intricacy, recording life's common-place details (the earmarks of a proper canoe; a raccoon's creaturely descent from a tree) as seen by a canny, gleaming eye despite passing shadows. Poetry is not just a matter of form but a habit of insight, and White's has snuck into impressively cramped, apparently anonymous quarters.

Another predatorial poetic instinct of his was to make a list. White tended to itemize scenes of gluttony and carnage with a matter-of-fact insouciance that avoided coming to any overweening moral conclusion. The saturation of garbage, say, in a barnyard or a fairground was enough to restore his spirits, if he could describe its overripe luxuriance briskly and simply.

To capture character in the flicker of an action, and in the flicker of a verb to equal it, was another favorite strategy. White's laconic preference was strangely effective and lankily mirthful.

A perfectly realized tone meant whimsy was allowable and affectation wasn't. This lesson is especially tricky.

Another: he could forget his worries and think about a piglet as a piglet would, if it could. (Negative capability.)

"Parvum opus" was a term he coined on behalf of someone else, but it applied well and positively to him. He thrived as a writer on the useful small parts of things. Words, punctuation, syntax, and informal rules of tongue were small enough, and they were useful. The smallest of all, as some poets know, can be the most germinal.

The smallest and most germinal is best shown when there is least of it to see. "Omit needless words!" a teacher had advised him, and White enthusiastically did.

His sense of humor was stealthy but well-mannered. He cared for the motor tenderhandedly. I'm unsure of what this has to do with poetry, since so few poems now are both humorous *and* earnest. Perhaps more of them should be.

He was fast, and he was gracious. Poetry is partly the craft of fashioning invisible transitions from thing to thing and thought to thought. White's observations of speed as a symptom of life in New York flit like Art Deco figures across the ice rink of the page.

⧖

YET THESE QUALITIES of White's aren't enjoying a full expression or fair impact as I grope for them. The poet in him was an extremist, even if the journalist wasn't. Extremism will briefly guide each of us, now.

My direct contact with this stylist has been ruddy, fraught, revealing. White has tempted me to put aside everything else, because his single-minded intensity, however clean and crisp the sentences, has been bombarding me. It's like this. On a chilly March evening after the monotonous forward zigzag of an industrious day, who wouldn't like to sit down on a *hot* dictionary? Having cooked in a history, the words in the book are ready to sting and sustain us, as White's are. Some people may require the intake of a fierce sparsity—selected syllables—through their wan, wintry pores.

Not a very Whitean sentence at all!

I so regret being literary. Wise to the literary compulsion, and resisting it successfully, he didn't need to regret anything—or need to be literary. Poetry doesn't need to be "literary," either, a fact that tantalizes me about White and helps to lure me to him.

But regardless, one danger of literary influence is the unpredictable outcome. If I am nagged now and again by this punctilious mind, he may mean only the best, and yet be ill-served in the end. His usefulness depends as much on me as on him.

All influences worth having must be cunning, like his, to undermine your opposition. The process of becoming influenced is parlous, a belligerent romancing. The protagonists must also be antagonists. After all, you'd have little to gain from a mere, safe, congenial second self. He needs to be different or estranging. It isn't sweet or fitting to serve your own interests, really. You need to be contradicted. You've almost got to seek out someone who won't bother to respect you. I know I deserve no respect from E. B. White.

Sometime, will I feel compelled to mumble, late at night, to a stupefied sleeper?

# The Poetry of Goats

WHEN WE WERE ABOUT FIVE and seven, my brother and I were given Kitzel, a goat. I don't remember having seen any goat before then, so it was as if she had been freshly invented for us. Few of her body parts were placed quite where we had expected them to be, subtly adjusted or altered for the goat's geometry.

For one thing, the hairs seemed so linear, running straight and undistracted like shingle, though in their droves of paths they didn't all face the same way. While the white and brown fur on the neck swam downward in neat, decisive strokes, vertically entranced, a whole big patch on the stomach formed a circular whorl, a sort of mystical happening. We liked petting that. Her ankles seemed almost feathered, so close in did the hairs gather there, gloving her mute tendon and bone. Fur in the lanes near the knotty joint in her leg — I'm not sure it should be called a knee — tried to fill in a space that looked abstruse and concave. The effort of filling it might be a little futile, forlorn. And so on across the entire animal — fields and tides of the rough, spiky presence, easily blown, the only tenderness, perhaps, that you could get out of a goat.

Her eyes were oblong, a curiosity that never stopped interesting us. The pupils and irises, of course, were oblong, too. This gave Kitzel's gaze an oddly concentrated look, as though, spread out like that, her sight were seeping, instead of looking. But because the eyes were also both narrow and bound, she gave the feeling of a scientist scrutinizing whatever was in front of her. I remember we wondered whether the anomalous shape of her eyes might be influencing the shape of what she saw, translating it into a confident, sturdy limbo.

⚔

DESCRIPTION IS NOT JUST a seduction, though I often ask myself why I feel so compelled to indulge in it. The goat brings up the question for me, because I want very much to describe her as she was when she first astonished us, but so do botanical facts—the lie of leaves, the way seeds organize themselves—seem to wait for me, or someone else, to describe them. Seeing can be a fixation in life (it has been for me), and to deny that would be to close my eyes and retreat. I sometimes wonder, though, if anyone or anything else feels exactly the hunger of eye that I uncomfortably feel—whether, for example, another eye would ever feed on me. If it did, and if I knew that, I would have no idea what to give it, what to leave behind as my evidence for the eye. All I seem to know about is my need.

Part of my fascination with description belongs to the apparent lie of it: to describe is not the same as to understand. Description is only description, a list of things witnessed, and when. Or, so we have sometimes assumed. Yet this isn't really so, can't be. Too much description, or the kind that is a sham—conducted as a dance on surfaces—very soon becomes empty. A better kind of description is never only factual or reportorial, and rarely light in manner. This kind comes as a personal symptom of perception let slip by the observer, given as a sign of who she is, whether or not she observes *it*, whether or not she likes revealing herself in public.

⚒

ALSO FASCINATING IS THE thing observed—the goat, I mean.

We loved ours right away, my brother and I, because Kitzel could be no one except herself. She didn't know how. There were other goats, but not another one of her—and she wasn't even aware of that. She was innocent of her own design. And the design was so matter-of-factly ingenious, so classically deviant. As an architect by training, my father especially enjoyed her. Unlike a building, our goat could move, and the movement helped to demonstrate the pugnacious efficiency of her design. At least, that is what I supposed he thought when he gazed at her with a bemused small grin. To watch her was an architectural fantasy, like imagining the Empire State Building out taking a jaunt.

Her habits seemed particularly intended to show off aspects of her design, as though to onlookers, trade apprentices. There was her basic gait, for instance: a deceptively stiff-legged strut, as if she had all the time in the world and no remarkable desire to make any use of it. While she took her tough, hardy little steps, lifting up from her high-heeled hooves, her tail winked freakishly, as if battery-powered, and her lackadaisical ears twitched. All the sitting down and rising were also interesting, a bit of a production, although adroit. There would arrive a moment in the folding up of her accessories—those pretend knees, rigid as a praying mantis's, the bulky body, and the little whirring tail-sprout—there would come a moment in her routine gambit of kneeling down in the grass (or of rebounding from it) when it looked like the whole thing wouldn't work. To succeed was visually improbable. The contraption of goat would have to topple. The feral elegance, always a bit risky, would simply escape the apparatus. Her archaic flavor would knock her over, like a sphinx let loose in Detroit.

Her successes, repeated, we took as the mark of a timeless intelligence.

⚒

YES, IT IS NECESSARY to go on with this: I'm sure to learn something from all the describing, itemizing, refining, and remembering, because the goat is a symbol to me, put in our midst to make a reckless statement, to improve our posture, to give us new ideas, to redecorate our stupid human prejudices. She existed beyond likelihood, and so was able to challenge it, clambering with obscure glee to her casual peak.

Her favorite peak was actually the car. She strode over and mounted it every so often, never leaving even a dent in her wake. Grace belongs to goats; it is a solid thing, graspable. They are carefree about it and not apt to abuse the talent, because they are not even slightly conscious of it. They just boggle on, happy to juice the weeds.

Sometimes she needed to drink. She did it in her own way, of course, like a marvelous sucking machine, her lipless muzzle opened just a notch, rhythmically summoning the tidal inch. Little by little, the water level in her pail swayed and lowered, in a frisky disappearing act.

It was also educational to watch Kitzel's alert gizmo self vying with a tree for lunch. Her chin zealously thrust, she would bite the branch, yank it close, then gobble all the stuff she could, bobbing her head affirmatively. No matter what came her way, she was never discouraged. Her broad, firm neck seemed to be her center, the pith of her strength. The stumpy horns helped to top it off with their brief, gnarled frenzy, and the wattles also somehow helped.

Wattles were a pair of soft, furry pelts ornamenting her neck in front with a mild panache, their original use unknown. Maybe primeval goats had worn them once as pendants; maybe the old wattles were painted a bright, vigilant hue. Even nowadays, her whited, colorless wattles tagged Kitzel, looping with a fairy license to the buried trove of her vocal cords underneath, as the essential goat she was and would be. The cords were frequently in use, though not indiscreet. They had a quality of risible mumble—a friendly, slowed, eaten buzz. Or, when heard at a higher volume, her voice roiled in an ancient, consoling vibrato.

⚒

WE ENVIED OUR GOAT HER wattles, I most of all, because the wattles were so pointlessly pretty and joyful—just the kind of thing to win over a panel of gods sitting in professional judgment. Long ago, wowed by the wattles, that committee had cast a vote decidedly in favor of all goats. Since then, her wattles had roused their warmest wishes on Kitzel's behalf.

Beyond decoration, wattles have no function; they seemed proof of the fact that she didn't need to do, only be. (Unlike the rest of us.) Her wattles were not going to be taken away, emended, outdated, eclipsed, or put to work in the future course of evolution. Kitzel had already earned her natural justification. She was impeccably designed; nature was lucky to have her. She was canny, courageous. The pelts were *her* sort of poem.

When we fed her each night before bed, dodging split-tailed bugs squirming through our handfuls of coarse grain (she never seemed to mind them), there could be no one more singularly at home with herself than Kitzel was. She had nowhere else to go but her body's eccentric house, and she lived there contentedly.

I wasn't sure at the time why Kitzel led me to goats as the unavoidable subject of my very first poem, but now I think I understand: a writer should find as sure a roost in a poem as a goat discovers in the trust of her hooves, wattles, spine, fur, sprite-tail, unfurling throat, and quizzical glance.

# The Wit of William Matthews

ONE OF THE THINGS WRONG with contemporary poetry: in a poem meant to be taken seriously, you'll probably never find a talking pig.

This may hurt the poetry. The lack of redeeming lowlife in upper-echelon literature — and in verse that is earnestly aspirant — imposes a limit on the writing and on the reader. So does the general absence of a sense of humor in much poetry written recently. These limits are unnecessarily uncomfortable and unrealistic.

By humor I don't mean easy laughs or exclusive lightness. Humor can bring newfound emotional dimension and the expansive influence of reason to a poem; it encourages people to stop thinking only about themselves. In a relaxed state of mind — and humor is a reliable relaxant — you are better able to entertain more various thoughts. Wit also helps you to think with a fuller clarity. When you are amused, contradictions feel accessible and friendly; imagination can be indulged, for a while, with fewer restraints and fears. The tragic sense also tends to burgeon, eventually, under the influence of mirth.

Especially when it mingles with the serious, funny writing—though exceptional now—can magnetize: James Tate's virtuoso absurdist whimsy; Marianne Moore's austere, deluxe, shyly scathing version of something akin to that; sardonic wits, like those of Byron and J. D. McClatchy; Frank O'Hara's exuberance, flushed and gabby, yet well defended by irony.

Humor can also go farther afield than our usual expectations permit. For instance, when I read some of the work of W. H. Auden and Emily Dickinson, the quality of asperity, flickering through two otherwise utterly different kinds of poetry, does not cause me to lose my head, but rattles my mind in a way I like. The asperity is a playful form of alertness (and a kind of moral chastening, too).

At another extreme, when I enjoy e. e. cummings, it's partly because he has the courage to be merrily, haphazardly bouffant in his manner with words. Humor breaks rules that seriousness can't. Because it's antiheroic, it can get away with a lot.

☒

HUMOR'S CAPACITY FOR SPEED and surprise has been honed by poets for a long time. One of the participants in that serious game was William Matthews, whose penultimate book, *Time and Money* (Houghton Mifflin, 1995), received the National Book Critics Circle Award. When I talked with him in 1996, Matthews was at work and at play on a translation of Horace's *Satires*.

"Life is far too serious not to be taken lightly," he suggested, with a pithiness that he may or may not have picked up during time spent with Martial, whose epigrams portraying life in first-century Rome he had translated. "To see oneself as struggling and funny at the same time is the richer and more complicated view,"

Matthews believed. "At its best, wit in poetry represents a kind of balance. It represents a skepticism. It represents the possibility that what makes you most earnest and serious is, perhaps, ridiculous.

"Earnestness and wit," he cautioned, "are sometimes thought to be mutually exclusive. A danger of earnestness is that one becomes the protagonist of one's own poems, and takes oneself far too seriously. Too great an earnestness allows only a huge, struggling protagonist: Somebody-Or-Other-Agonistes. The agony is real enough, and the ridiculousness of the agony is real enough, and wit accommodates the interplay between those two in a way that straightforward seriousness doesn't."

In the balancing act performed by wit in poetry, what purpose is served by light verse?

"An enormous amount of light verse is like popcorn," Matthews commented. "Light verse *sets out* to be funny. A more serious poetry, lit ruefully from within by wit, has not set out to be funny, but has discovered itself to be in a hilarious predicament. The sense of predicament seems to me absent from most light verse. Its goal is to make a humorous pattern. A problem with the best of light verse — though I suppose it is also one of the pleasures — is that much of the humor is about form. I'm thinking of Ogden Nash, where two lines will rhyme, but one line will be seventeen syllables long and the other will be three, and the joke is about the anxiety that form provokes. In a lot of light verse, it's the same joke over and over again — which is that form will make a kind of meaning, whether you want it or not, and the meaning will be faintly ridiculous. Light verse could be said to have the opposite problem of earnest verse. Earnest verse wants very much to be terribly serious, and can wind up being unintentionally funny; light verse sets out to be very funny, and can wind up being leaden.

"Wit should be an instrument of poise. What's humorous should be discovered, rather than sought."

Matthews's discovery of Horace dated to his boyhood, when he read the Roman poet "rather haltingly, in Latin, much aided by existing translations." The wit of the writer was the draw. "Horace uses wit as a kind of gyroscope, as a way of moving swiftly and interestingly without driving off the road and cracking up. Of all the poets I can think of, in any of the languages and traditions I have access to, Horace is the best example of how that works. There's an affectionate interest in the world, the world as it's constituted now, rather than, as in Martial's case, in the world as it *ought* to have been. And that directed affection for the world is not as usual in poetry as one might think. Horace understands how poorly we have done some of the things we might have done to be human. He is ever cognizant of those, but also able to say to himself, 'This tragedy is ordinary'—for better or for worse. Part of what's attractive is that he knows humans well enough not to be especially startled by anything they do. He had a deeply pragmatic sensibility, not the sensibility of a believer or a holder of positions."

For readers of Matthews, such observations may also seem to have characterized this poet's natural inclinations, though Matthews seemed to feel less certain of the implicit affinities.

"Friends of mine have said, 'Gee, Horace seems perfect for you,' and I've always thought to myself, 'This *can't* be right.' What's required of a translator is some sense of sympathetic vibration—that your tuning forks are going at about the same speed. But also some sense of difference and distance, something that you have to overcome or develop in yourself in order to make a more adequate impersonation of the other party. I don't believe it's at all the case that you're attracted to translate someone because it's a perfect match. This marriage was not made in heaven, but in Hoboken."

Still, what made the match?

"Friendship, pleasure, food, and conversation are important things for me," he replied. "It seems to me that if poetry could be described as having a 'subject,' it could be pleasure. Pleasure is one of the truest human subjects, and one that's not addressed very directly in poetry. One of the things that's appealing about Horace is that he's interested in these questions.

"Horace was a worldlier man than Martial and had a very different career in Rome. He was genial, successful. A lot of his friends were people who were routinely used to accumulating and exercising power. And Horace didn't think that was necessarily a bad thing. Given his urbanity, the pleasures of the dinner table and the pleasures of watching the folly of one's fellow humans—including oneself—were at least as important as warfare and politics.

"Almost all of the *Satires* are a drama of some kind. Some are a single drama told from beginning to end; some are a series of linked and related anecdotes or minidramas. Somebody comes to dinner and things go hilariously wrong. Several people are trotted out as examples of excessive greed—people who, when they reach a point of prosperity and equilibrium, can't stop amassing more stuff, and ruin their lives and the lives of the people around them. Horace is amused at all the excesses, and participates in them by making them up and satirizing them, and keeps a distance from them at the same time. He gets to impersonate all the way through the satire, then disassociates himself. He becomes everybody—he is all of his characters, briefly. He was also slowly exploding the notion received from the

Greeks that there were particular meters appropriate to particular kinds of poems. So that one of Horace's missions was to extend the range of rhetorical and metrical modes that were available for a given poem and to show that he knew all the Greek rules and could replace or loosen them.

"The *Satires* are essaylike. They have something in common with Montaigne, perhaps the most Horatian of writers in the later European tradition. And some of Emerson's essays are related to the way Horace's poems work. Poetry did all these different things in Horace's period, and had not given up or had stolen from it much of the territory that is now in the possession of prose. His public agreed to be mildly rebuked or agreed to have its follies and enthusiasms called into question. This was like the situation now of the professional comic, which to us means stand-up comics or writers of comic scripts. In fact, in one of the *Satires*, Horace says, 'Well, I'm not really writing great poetry. This is a kind of inky talk' — or, that's how I translate it. The *Satires* are relaxed, they're longer, they're more discursive, they're social and public, and they don't have the compressed private lyricism that some of Horace's odes have."

By way of example, Matthews spoke of the plot of a satire he had not yet finished translating, involving "a disastrous dinner party. The host has left the room because things have gone so horribly. He weeps at one point. He brings out all these arcane dishes to save the dinner, which is already in ruins. A wall hanging falls down onto this great fish dish that was supposed to be the pièce de résistance, and not only breaks the platter the fish is on, but all the dirt that had gathered in the folds of the wall hanging gets all over the fish and the table. The dinner is *not* saved. The guests are in absolute rebellion, and they flee.

They don't eat anything! And as they're fleeing, they say, 'We're fleeing for revenge!' Revenge for the host's pretention; revenge for his being a public failure. There's a certain amount of cruelty to this satire. This guy's a jerk, but he's humiliated in the poem past a level that would be comfortable to live with afterward, if this were a real dinner. And probably it was based on a real dinner."

The hilarity of satire, however, wasn't all fun and games for Matthews the translator. Comic "inky talk" may be tougher to translate than straight-faced verse, he proposed.

"The challenge in translating Horace was partly technical," he explained. "To write 140 lines of poetry in a satire, even when you're given an absolutely brilliant original—to talk about human behavior in ordinary ways, as opposed to human behavior when you go down into the underworld, or lash yourself to a mast to avoid being lured to your death by the Sirens... those passages about the Sirens and the underworld may perhaps be easier to write. So part of the fun is to wonder, 'Can I do this? Can I write well enough to maintain Horace's kind of unbroken suction between the poem and the reader?'

"His poems are incredibly swift. While they toy with being didactic and philosophical, they're in fact extraordinarily fast. I've adopted a flexible blank verse line, which runs somewhere between eight and twelve syllables; it's an accordiony blank verse. You're sort of on this escalator, trying to get the pace right, get the tone right, and not make it seguey and anecdotal. The pace and the ease of the *Satires* are the hardest things about them."

Even when his work on Horace was nearly completed, to take a retrospective view of it seemed dangerous. "I don't *want* the last of the work on the manuscript to be complicated by my sense of what I may have gained or lost from doing the translations,"

Matthews declared nervously. "The last thing you know about it is what it did to *you*. But I'm convinced that part of the appeal of the translation enterprise is that you believe, in some strange way, that you will be changed by it. It's not just that you fall in love because you like being in love and you really adore the other person. You also fall in love because you think you will become a slightly different person, and more interesting to yourself with that partner."

When everything's done, "it's certainly true that a body of work is a body of play," Matthews noted. "But poets are forever anxious. They believe they're doing something central to life, investigating the relationship between language and emotion. Most of the culture, though, thinks we're doing something extraordinarily trivial, that we're almost anachronistic. So 'body of work' gives off a nice Calvinistic ring. Whereas 'body of play' confirms the suspicion that our culture already has about poetry — that it's a kind of mud-pie activity."

# Stealing Glimpses

My last encounter with the poet A. K. Ramanujan took place as we were riding on a train headed for downtown Chicago. I remember the scene through the window as though I had invented it: tumbledown industrial outskirts, the quaintly gracious backyard stretches of a few museums, and the Zen hint of Lake Michigan in its pearly storehouse.

Smudgily speckled sunflowers usually flourished, during the right season, near the railroad tracks and in other agreeably neglected barrens. As I rode the train, I was picturing them, though they hadn't yet sprouted; it would be July before the weight and conscience of a humid midwestern summer could force them to bloom.

Isn't it strange to be seduced by a flower that hasn't yet flowered? Perhaps, though, it's a morning state of mind. No one has had time, so far, to appraise you, and you owe nothing to them. You're only half present even to yourself, and the condition is a relief. You're susceptible—and serene.

In fact, I didn't much want to be reminded of where I was or who I was, but when Raman suddenly appeared in the aisle of the train, of course I asked him to sit beside me.

Raman impressed me with his physically quiet way of conducting himself from spot to spot. He seemed to glide and settle, not to walk, as though his mind "worked" and his person emanated after it. He was one of those rare people who spent a good deal of his life listening, to others or himself. That morning, especially, he seemed clothed in a listener's stance: an unjudgmental, reposeful, peering position. He was a nonaggressor in a quite aggressive city.

Since we shared a milieu—the University of Chicago—as well as various friends, but had rarely talked alone, at first silence met with silence on the train.

For me at the time, conversation usually concerned grades, news, weather, moods, proofs, books, or a controversy racking an editor or a writer. Instead, Raman and I talked about the need to look out of windows.

We agreed that writing was rather like looking out of windows—the page (or the screen) was a kind of window. And a real window functioned somewhat like a page: the setting beyond it swarmed with an appealing potential. You looked aimlessly, and then with a growing sense of purpose that slowly offered itself.

Why was it necessary to look?

To enjoy contact without commitment, one might answer. Or, to contemplate possibilities. To dream the life of a poem as it's lived outside of you, before you can write it. (Arch, but still accurate.) Or maybe, to abandon yourself and obey your eyes, instead.

Regardless, the point of looking was freedom: the freedom not to expect any view in particular, and to actually savor a loss of dominion over your surroundings. To let the outer become inner, and the inner outer, at a sultry pace.

One of the consequences of our conversation was that I no longer regretted all my time previously given to the hapless gaze.

Raman mostly listened. I—uncharacteristically—monopolized the talking. And we both kept stealing glimpses of our common "beyond" streaming by past the train window. The window itself did not provide much in the way of ideas. But the conversation shifted, so that we began to recognize how active the habit of looking can be.

The shift came about when Raman chose to compare the human liking for staring into space with a spider's disposition to spin. Of course, a finished web proves that an appetite has led to something—and a blank look may not lead anyplace. But he continued, speaking with admiration for the spider, who knew innately how to make the thing, and who was both more skillful and less doubtful than a writer.

However, Raman noted, if a spider were treated with hallucinogens, then the pattern of the web and the manner of its creation had to alter. They were subject to good and bad influences.

What happened to the web? I asked him.

And he described with elegant gusto how asymmetrical and disheveled a web could be. I enjoyed the paradox of his elliptical precision in speech and the billowing tatters of gauzy production. The spider, he said, would seem unaware of the change in his or her craftmanship. And Raman evinced greater interest in a web that had been disturbed than in one that was perfect.

As he observed or imagined it, the hallucinogenic web was magnificent because it was subject to deranged urges. Perhaps it was more metaphysically truthful than any well-ordered artifact could be. This web was no longer a model or an icon. But it was an accurate record of life, because destruction was tangled up in it.

Of course, a deranged web was also more difficult to look at, requiring a kind of connoisseurship very different from what we were used to.

Imagine the kinds of details that would clamor for attention in such a web: gaping holes. Smaller omissions. Veerings. A refusal to give a script. An extreme yen for pattern, countered by a severe insurgence. Graphic ambivalence.

No word was said of inscribing our wishes and needs on a window or on the vistas visible through glass. And yet, a devoted observer is an artist, as a spider is. We can't help but alter what we glimpse as we glimpse it.

Even so, our desires, acuities, and means are largely invisible to us. And so, how tempting it can be to make something more of these than observation would allow, then disrupt that, fish for the intentions, guess at the prospects—create and derange, again and again.

Raman is no longer living, but I think fairly often of the window and his spiders.

# Poets and Their Friends

How many poems were first written primarily for friends, or were inspired by them? My unproven suspicion is that poets may rely more closely than other creative people on sympathetic peers to serve as editors and critics—to heat, share, inhabit, or qualify the process of writing. If that is so, then in poetry friendship is matchless.

Why would this be? Within literature, poetry is often regarded as a specialty, whether by poetry's adversaries or well-wishers. The language and the literary conduct are understood as distinct, and both are puzzling at times to "prosers" (poet and memoirist Mary Karr's word). So if poetry is less welcoming to the many than to the few, the few may cluster together, despite their feints and antipathies.

That passion sustains poetry is a commonplace, a baffling inevitability. (Why should it?) Put some poets together in a room for an hour or two, and more than a few will emerge with inflamed feelings afterward. (For "passion" a novelist friend of mine substitutes "oversensitivity.") Passion can work for the bad or the good. But friendship is its best possible outcome.

Friendship offers pragmatism and an ideal: a way to live with someone else while imagining an even better way. The habit of friendship is comparatively stable, even when impassioned, and should be able to absorb or withstand the intemperate abandon and the crazing changes of luck or letters. Friendship is more realistic than extreme forms of love, and can help to preserve you. Poetry is not a bad preservative, either.

&#10005;

A NUMBER OF BOOKS bearing on poetic friendships have shown in recent years how complex and yet durable friendship's bonds can be.

"I am wondering," wrote twenty-four-year-old Elizabeth Bishop to her friend Marianne Moore in 1935, "if you have seen Martin Johnson's moving picture *Baboons?* It *looks*, from the previews, as if it might have in it a few very nice animals, and I am planning to go and see it. If you haven't seen it already, I wonder if you would care to go with me one afternoon this week? It is so cold that going out is very uncomfortable, but I should like so much to take you if you could consider it. I could meet you at the theatre any afternoon except Thursday, at any time convenient for you. I have had my eye on another animal film called, I think, *Sequoia*, but it doesn't sound quite as promising as *Baboons*."

Ingenuously diplomatic, this paragraph from Bishop's letter suggests her spirited respect for the elder stateswoman of poetry, and in a very few lines characterizes their joint affinity, one that lasted for as long as they did. Few biographers could handle the hotness or the lightness of the implied exchange between the two, or its fetching quotidian quality. Bishop's letters, which often elaborate on her friendships with poets, seem to share the same ink as poetry's. They are collected in *One Art*, edited by Robert Giroux (Farrar, Straus and Giroux, 1994).

In reading about poets and friendships, you want the right witness to be reporting—someone honest, attentive, probing, and not mirthless. David Kalstone's critical tact recommends him for the role in *Becoming a Poet* (Farrar, Straus and Giroux, 1989), a thoughtful exploration of overlapping allegiances among Bishop, Moore, and Robert Lowell in friendships waged partly with and for poetry.

A more personal tact guides Eileen Simpson, former wife of John Berryman, in *Poets in Their Youth* (Random House, 1982), her memoir of their marriage and their friendships with poets Randall Jarrell, R. P. Blackmur, Lowell, Allan Tate, and others. Simpson's concern is the suffering encountered by a generation of American poets who knew and cared for one another but could not stave off individual misery either together or alone. She doesn't monger in misery, though it ignited the poetry. Simpson's sanity leaves an impression of appropriate muted wit while she tells the story of a slow-moving, prolonged catastrophe.

Even so, "Poets in their skins will never equal their poems," Donald Hall once declared in an essay, concluding a persuasively impious comment on Robert Frost. ("The man on the platform, the man at the cocktail party, was vain and vulnerable, needed adulation, needed victory," he wrote of Frost.) To understand a poet, even when the poet is a friend, one should begin with the writing, not the life. Hall is a more acerbic observer of poets and poet-friends than Kalstone or Simpson, but he excels in critical portraiture: his authority comes from the shrewd squint of a peer's pore-to-pore judgment. The irascible intimacy of his opinions can end by revealing his own sensibility, as much as anyone else's. For Hall at his most perceptive, consult his evocative character study of Dylan Thomas in *Their Ancient Glittering Eyes: Remembering Poets and More Poets* (Ticknor & Fields, 1992). This foray into the other poet's many charms, his drunkenness and solecisms, and his self-doubts is ultimately more frank, generous, and seemingly accurate than any.

Just as intimate, if more kaleidoscopic in scale, is Peter Davison's grapple with the formative flux of poetic activity in Boston from 1955 to 1960 in *The Fading Smile* (Knopf, 1994). Like Simpson's, his book offers a generational group portrait, and his narration is poignantly quickened by his sense of urgency as a poet and an editor of poets with whom he seems umbilically associated: Hall, Plath, Rich, Kunitz, Wilbur, Sexton, Lowell, Merwin, et al. Explains Davison in his first chapter, "I believe there is one thing my generation seems to have had in common: nearly all of us had had in life to struggle with our fathers; and now our fathers-in-poetry were themselves dying." He adds later, "I had inherited—that is the only word—a passion for poetry, and an awe of its power so overmastering that I was paralyzed by a resistance to becoming a maker of poems." The tectonic wrench that had to take place as a result was the means by which poems were written there and then. Maybe only Davison, as a crony and a critic of all concerned, could tell us so.

☓

YET FOR THE STRENGTH and span of his friendships, perhaps no poet in our century distinguished himself more than W. H. Auden. A famously lonesome man, he cultivated company.

Especially in the years since his death in 1973, Auden's friends and collaborators have exulted in his memory, while seeming to raise the stakes for friendship and for writing. To Hannah Arendt, for example, Auden appeared "an expert in the infinite varieties of unrequited love." (Though he was gay, he proposed marriage to her. She declined.) His brother John saw in him "an isolation and sadness which arose from his uprooted and solitary existence." Friendship represented one sort of morality for Auden, perhaps the main one; poetry represented another.

The writer Oliver Sacks, a friend to Auden, has described the poet's "genius for friendship" and his "extraordinary powers of sympathy and empathy," embodied not only in friendship itself but in the further idea of "cosiness." In *W. H. Auden: A Tribute* (Macmillan, 1975), edited by Stephen Spender, Sacks remarks on how

words became palpable, solid, alive, when Wystan used them, both things in themselves and expressions of himself: and this was especially true of the word "cosy." He cared nothing for possessions as such; they only had meaning for him as vehicles of personal meaning and feeling. The first time I had tea with him—back in 1969—I found the teapot in a tea-cosy, and my egg in an egg-cosy; and this was in no sense mere eccentricity or oddity—Wystan put them in cosies because he cared for them personally—they ceased to be mere things, inanimate, and were given a life and reality of their own: he would say "you" to the teapot, as Goethe said "you" to the stone. When he saw me out—I had a BMW at the time, with a jacketed tank—he was pleased at the sensible and simple design of the machine (this was Wystan the boy, the lover of models and mines and machines, of good craftsmanship of every kind) but he was especially taken by the jacket round the tank: "I like that," he said, "it shows you care for the bike. I have never seen a bike with a bike-cosy before. But it's absolutely right—it belongs where it is."

Sacks goes on to compare the cosiness of the bike-cosy with Auden's "cosiness of language itself, the fitting together of words and ideas . . . the way in which every word is . . . encysted, nested cosily in its right and proper place, where it belongs, at home." Even those who question Auden's attachment to metrical felicity and his occasional urge to orate may admire his drive to construct a precision from precariousness—to find a home in verse.

As his friend Thekla Clark has reminded us in her memoir, *Wystan and Chester* (Columbia University Press, 1996), Auden didn't really have a home until late in life when, with money from a literary prize, he bought a house outside Vienna in Kirchstetten in 1957. This home magnetized his friends as not even his New York City digs had done. For the British-born poet, who was disparaged by the English when he left for America in the gathering hell of World War II, it hadn't been easy to find a place to stay put. But Auden lived in Kirchstetten during the warm months for sixteen years with Chester Kallman, his virtual spouse.

Left to his own devices, Auden had the housekeeping habits of a nitwitted waif. Recalled composer Nicolas Nabokov, who collaborated with librettists Auden and Kallman on the opera *Love's Labour's Lost*, "[Auden's] flat is pervaded by a permanent stink of cat piss." That was in New York. Robert Craft, who worked as Stravinsky's assistant when Auden and Kallman were writing the libretto for *The Rake's Progress*, remembered that the poet "came to rehearsals in a white linen suit polka-dotted in front with Chianti stains." Dorothy Farnan, who eventually married Kallman's father, wrote that "Wystan and Chester's apartments and houses alike always had the appearance of a carpenter's shop gone awry or a public building about to be vacated. . . . The floors were never swept. If one took up a broom to help out, Chester would raise his wrist to his brow with a pained expression and say, 'Pul-eeze! Do not raise the dust.'. . . In the past, Wystan had set out food at night for his favorite mouse."

Kirchstetten was different. A seemly Austrian came in regularly to clean. Clark describes the household cocktail schedule (rather rigid) and their adventures in sausage cuisine ("We made a miscalculation and the quantities were so vast that Chester and I were up until one o'clock in the morning finishing the casings"). The air of caringly arranged foolery sounds like ideal summer larking.

Yet how larky could life have been for Auden and Kallman, who according to Humphrey Carpenter, one of Auden's biographers, had lost all of their sexual rapport in 1941? Especially since publication of Clark's memoir, some have rated Auden and Kallman as exemplars of the best in gay marriage; Clark provides the first convincing double portrait of the men. Their union, though, may have been most redemptive for its failure and their own persistent resilience. To her credit, Clark observes frictions and imbalances, bringing Kallman to the foreground as an urbane and generous charmer whose sporadic desire to lose everything was muscled to a temporary halt by his much older mate, the financial provider. But Auden gave voice more eloquently in his poetry to the humbling tribulations of this, his most important friendship.

Less than a month after meeting Kallman, then a Brooklyn College student, in 1939, Auden was telling friends that he expected "marriage" to come of their romance. Two years later, however, Kallman was unfaithful to him. Auden learned of it, and Kallman apparently bowed out of his sexual role, unwilling to submit to Auden's monogamous standards. Only after their relationship changed did Auden and Kallman begin working on a series of collaborative libretto projects; it was Kallman who had won Auden over to the pleasures of opera. The poetry of each writer continued to reflect the other, and Auden helped Kallman to be published.

Auden's poem "In Sickness and in Health," written in 1940, includes this stanza.

> Let no one say I Love until aware
> What huge resources it will take to nurse
>     One ruining speck, one tiny hair
> That casts a shadow through the universe:
> We are the deaf immured within a loud
> And foreign language of revolt, a crowd
> Of poaching hands and mouths who out of fear
> Have learned a safer life than we can bear.

Twenty-three years afterward, in "Thanksgiving for a Habitat," Auden dedicated the concluding section of the poem, "The Common Life," to Kallman, and observed there how some of us, bound to intimates,

> manage to forgive impossible behavior,
>     to endure by some miracle

conversational tics and larval habits
without wincing (were you to die,
I should miss yours).

The intentional modesty of the poetry solders stronger feeling to the lines than the speaker will overtly allow.

A fair number of his poems were either dedicated to Auden's friends or given less formally to them. In his tribute to Auden, Oliver Sacks reveals his emotion on finding certain favorite words of his own tucked knowingly by Auden into poems, like messages in bottles sent furtively and fondly from one writer to another. Were the poems at times dressed in their cosies? Not sentimentally, but to mark mutual affection, a propriety, a link.

Clark refers in her book to an early version of "For Friends Only," the poem Auden wrote for her and her husband, both of whom visited him often in Kirchstetten. In his *Collected Poems* (Random House, 1976), the two essential stanzas of the poem are these:

Easy at first, the language of friendship
Is, as we soon discover,
Very difficult to speak well, a tongue
With no cognates, no resemblance
To the galimatias of nursery and bedroom,
Court rhyme or shepherd's prose,

And, unless often spoken, soon goes rusty.
Distance and duties divide us,
But absence will not seem an evil

If it make our re-meeting
A real occasion. Come when you can:
Your room will be ready.

His poetry did much to establish a "tongue" for friendship—
a notion far more original (and more touching) than it sounds in
the abstract. One reason Auden so grips me may be his astute
reach beyond the limits of himself and the limits, even, of poetry.
This was a profoundly friendly reach.

Tellingly, biographer Humphrey Carpenter has noted Auden's
comparison of poems with chummy letters.

"All good art," [Auden] often declared, "is in the nature of
a letter written to amuse a sick friend. Too much art, par-
ticularly in our time, is only a letter written to oneself."

# True Confession

TEACHING AND LEARNING ARE TOO OFTEN kept separate, like two beliefs that can't mix, ordinarily. That's a shame, because most beliefs are somehow related; belief is, if nothing else, a unifier.

And poetry is nothing if not a belief. To teach it or to learn it is to discover unsuspected possibilities, based on old assumptions, and based also on independent bent and communal willingness. To pursue the belief is to withstand mass indifference, the tug of passing distractions, the urge to look for easier pleasures (if there really are any), and the claim of other responsibilities recognized more commonly. You have to rebuff reason to do that.

As a reader and a writer, I once believed that poetry could not be taught—only explained, discussed, rendered, and rerendered. The evidence? The classroom. Taking poetry apart was the typical class act. And it could be very useful, depending on who did the taking apart, who watched or listened, and how much further analysis would lead you after you left the room. Too often, though, you left with the bubbling dregs of an argument on your mind, not with poetry. Poetry had leached, had fled, seduced and abandoned by intellect.

Recently I discovered something different. Poetry can be taught, and can be learned.

I learned this long after I had almost forgotten what poetry was. I learned only after abandoning it. I learned as an improper acolyte, as one of the formerly faithful. I learned by chance. And I learned in a classroom.

They didn't just take poetry apart, my teachers. Then what did they do?

They taught as learners. But they knew better than we did how to learn. Their experience in learning intensified their interest and bred a surefooted humility. They showed us how to learn, but didn't tell us.

How different from the usual experience of a student. Instead of listening to a detached mind murmur, we watched someone summon strength from poetry. They wanted to share it. They considered things we might not have considered, big, rich, teetery. They were seeking. We were watching, and then joining in.

I was grateful to be taught like this. And yet, studying with these teachers was also unnerving. For I'd been dutifully following a narrow professional path without much poetry on it—and now, I realized, I might have to stop following. I would have to listen. I would probably need to change. And I did change.

Sometimes it is the job of a teacher to remind you of who you are, were, and who you might yet be. My teachers did that, even though I was a stranger to them. Their suggestive power was mysterious; it shook me like a wind. I have them to thank for part of my confusion, and I do thank them.

The return of a lost belief can raise doubt, cause pain. I don't understand why, but I feel it.

Was I wrong to have abandoned poetry when I did?

I don't remember abandoning it. Those early years aren't vivid. They were filled with work and were shaped by the deadlines and desires of editors. At the time, I was an editor, too, and whenever I wrote, I had to answer to another. I had faith in my dual role. As the professional logic went, my editing of other writers (and the editing of my own writing by editors) would preserve my sanity and improve my sentences, build objectivity and prevent the depravity of true confession in writing. Paragraphs, the editors believed, should exist as common property, and to become common properly they had to be cool and clear, conventional and heartless.

For all my monkeying then with style and signature in sentences, I did not want to confess. If confessing brings forgiveness, I certainly didn't want to be forgiven.

I wanted to be a construction worker with sentences. When each job was finished, it was finished, and I'd leave, paid, washing my hands.

I was paid for leaving the words behind, not for writing them; paid for allowing them to become faceless.

Naturally, I wasn't contented. My surroundings reeked of propriety and judiciousness. Things didn't get better — quite the contrary.

I was producing, repeating, and producing. I grabbed and did. I was a sophisticated literalist. (Now I hope I'm not one, though I do editing of another kind.)

I tried to use words artfully. I tried to make them serve a use, whatever that might be.

But do words care for their uses? They submit for a moment, then slip away to another purpose.

Possibly, it's better to be their servant.

What is service?

Maybe it's what I'm here to learn, as a reader or a writer, a teacher or a student.

# Squirming Cuneiform:
# When a Dance Is a Poem

I'M SCANNING A LIST of the Pilobolus Dance Theatre's repertoire dating from 1971, when this modern dance company was founded, to the present. The titles of the dances choreographed during those twenty-eight years seem poetically suggestive. When you read a lot of them, in or out of their chronological order, a verbal clot forms and plays with its own syllables like pseudo-podia. Try it.

*Albatross for Dinner*
*Eye of Samhain*
*Geode*
*Lost in Fauna*
*The Particle Zoo*
*Coming of Age in the Milky Way*
*Vestidigitations*

See what I mean? As a table of contents for a dance company, a repertoire can also sometimes cohere as a poem.

*The Particle Zoo* is one of my favorite titles ever, even when I agree to forget what the dance that is its namesake looks like. The title suggests cartoon plots that swarm around the three words, cellular and magisterial. Likewise, *Vestidigitations* is like a verbatim picture: an action seems implied that must be gigantic. And various suggestions bounce off each other on the list: the "eye" of Samhain, for instance, could really be a "geode." Or to come of age in the Milky Way, one might be required to eat an albatross for dinner. Especially in the heyday of our Magnetic Poetry sensibility, a list such as this one is likely to incite rearrangement, play, and tweaking, as though everyone could become a puzzle master, if not a poet.

For Pilobolus, the poetic analogy may lead further than for some dancers and dances. During a recent Pilobolus engagement in New York, I was reminded all over again of how much we tend to take imagery for granted on the street, in a poem, or on the stage. Instead of taking imagery for granted, Pilobolus takes it apart and reconfigures it, while seeming to let us in on the process. That's what makes the company's work distinct: the drama of exposure in a making is every dance's means of unfolding. The dancers bend the traditional dance vocabulary, intensifying the drama. Also, because Pilobolus has always functioned as a collective, the troupe seems to adjust organizational and creative hierarchies, giving art a relatively liberal, even artless profile. When dancers make contact in a Pilobolus piece, for example, whether frontal or elliptical, they do it informally, with a warmth that doesn't seem assumed or prepped, just lived. And when you watch their bodies construct (or deconstruct) a gymnastic architecture, it's like seeing Elizabethan script abandon the ceremonies and melt into a modernist incorrigibility.

The drama of exposure in the dances should not be neglected by us just for the fun of the gambits — and there are plenty of gambits. For instance, one of the company's best-known pieces, wittily called *Untitled* (1975), is a seeming comic allegory about matriarchs. The visual jokes are bulbous and endearing and cummings-like: two hugely tall Edwardian women shelter a nude man apiece under their voluminous skirts, though at first we don't know they are doing this; only the parenthetical flapping of the skirt eventually reveals the guy, all the hairier by contrast with the decorum of the dress billowing over him. The men act as the women's secret life stilts, raising and moving them through the mad plot of human endeavor, and incidentally helping to goad the piece's licentiously playful imagery. Exposure here allows for a juicy psychologizing to take place freely: women who need men who need women pass through unbelievable pratfalls, and they survive. The dance's surrealism is not political but contrary to politics, siding instead with anarchy. So outsize and ingenious is the danced stage scribble that the naked men gradually come to seem more clothed than the ladies, elaborately cushioned, a Victorian contrivance, the upholstered bod. Hadn't we invented the body before Pilobolus did?

Another kind of company exposure is typical of another sort of Pilobolus dance — the narrative sort, implied but never told outright. For a long time I've admired the way these storytelling pieces make their way through imagery alone, eschewing the code of usual gestures that tends to afflict dances, classical or modern. A standard-bearer of this sort is *Land's Edge* (1986), a dance for six that evokes an odd assortment of emotional states, en route to unwinding a tale of despair, mockery, whimsy, stoicism, more. The power of the imagery, approaching mime in its clarity of detail, is emotionally potent but also gains a second life and oomph from the quality of abstract verity that is achieved. The dancers' fineness of execution raises the standard for the image. Every particle matters, however small, and so the whole becomes complexly specific, engorged. Even if you drop the thread of the story, the spectacular refinement of what you see takes hold of you pristinely, like a formalism one can't do without. Offhand, I can't think of any poet able or inclined to do the same.

Pilobolus uses physical resources to improvise fresh lingos. Customs are not forgiven. You leave the theater after a Pilobolus performance wondering why the street lamps, fire hydrants, and scanty urban trees don't take leave of their senses to form outré geometries, as Pilobolus dancers do. Their dancing has dignity but likes mischief, drawling a squirming cuneiform that makes the body feel enjoyably, legibly unfamiliar. Poets could do worse than wish this lingo would infect them. In watching the dancers, we might pine to be translated into multilimbed, many-mouthed, prehensile observers—or just write like them.

# Ashbery's Stand-Up Comedy

READING HIM SILENTLY TO MYSELF, I hadn't realized at first the possibly amusing consequences of a sheerly oral, aural Ashbery. Then I listened again, with a different result. His own spoken delivery of the poems may be modest, reticent, or impersonal. Yet a more attuned delivery of Ashbery's poetry—attentive and responsive to the patterns of breath implied in his idiosyncratic patterns of consciousness—would resemble that of an intellectual patterer, who talks and pronounces, in part, to bulk up spare moments, to occupy an audience (almost any audience), and to assuage himself. The comic prepossessingness of Ashbery's speakers accrues from their ability to absorb time, or stick to time, without seeming to; their comic timing heals their mortality, at least in the short term. And their rush of verbal activity in Ashbery's poems is constantly vernal and renewing, exuberant in the performance.

Not everyone will be persuaded by my perception of Ashbery as a comic, let alone a stand-up comic (who would seem, by definition, to lack dignity). But to me he is comic and provisional in the same sense as Merce Cunningham and John Cage, who are also profoundly dignified. His comic touch represents an unfashionable inclusiveness in art, which normally shirks the comic.

Ashbery's performative prolixity on the page is an aspect of what may suggest his intriguingly antipoetic stance: he seems so wholesomely, unquestioningly oral, so unperturbed by the generous volume and the cousinly charms of his verbal orchestra. I am struck by his quality of flighty earnestness, by both the density and the dash of it, by the improvisational setting forth, and so forth, and so forth—by his knack for changing position or direction quickly, confidently, as though he were really continuing to wage an argument. Is he? In fact, the argument is so subject to change and variation that it doesn't resemble argument as we commonly understand this, in the sense of a "minded," rational progression. Rationality serves instead as a deceptive ruse in his "argument," as a brief, fleeting hint of formalism imposed on the grander, unkempt snarl or stream of a consciousness.

Part of the comedy derives from the seemingly unselected vastness of an Ashbery poem. He doesn't appear to choose (words, thoughts, lines): the results of his choices mass and gravitate (and levitate) with a pulse that seems their own. The mastermind has absented himself from their midst. Yet, you know he's there. This somewhat sly half-presence can magnetize all on its own, regardless of the verbal cascades, the patter that reaches a listener or reader first and foremost.

As a "comic," he can amuse only because he is intelligent. That is, unlike generic comics, Ashbery relies on no shtick; his lines are too lifelike. His poem "Daffy Duck in Hollywood" shows Ashbery's performative gusto and its range of consequences.

The poem claims and flaunts license early as a comedic and aesthetic creed: in the fourth line, "everything" is cited as a material substance and a bodiless experience that is "creeping across" (line one) the narrator. The "creeping" adventure grants Ashbery a libertine right to record further sensational plethora. He asserts the right through the coursing of the poem with an extravagant range of diction and allusion to encompass and satirize the "everything" that is encountered, that swarms. The energy brandished throughout the writing is youthful, reckless, and defiantly "pop." And yet, the well-witted speed of the narrative, implying an elastically constraining subterranean conflict, also seems maturely calculated to pierce Ashbery's élan. This dualism reminds me, if loosely, of the self-scathing common among stand-up comics, who seem to rely compulsively on hostility as a cue and a commodity in their seat-of-the-pants monologues.

Just what is the conflict implied by the poet-comic in this monologue? And how does the manic oral surge of the poem reveal the conflict by degrees? Without the conflict underneath, the poem's hurtling humor might seem frivolous, without a mortal "catch" — and then our figurative laughs would be few. Only the catch can cause hurt, and hurt (potential; real) is the basis for laughs, whether on Letterman or in Ashbery.

The conflict is implicit, I think, in the narrator's passive position with regard to experience, and in the poet's position with regard to the poem. The narrator is the one, perhaps the only one, to be crept upon. He submits to life's awful abundance, as Ashbery does to the poem's, but sooner or later must blow his top, rebel under pressure, and out come diction, allusion, mania, and poetry from him. Would the oppressed willingly rebel in much the same voice as the oppressor, in the very way that

Ashbery's narrator seems to? The true rebel insists on vocalizing with a deviant voice in critique of oppression. But Ashbery doesn't—hence, pain. To blow his top is still to submit, in a way. Of course, blowing one's top is also fun, granting a transgressive reprieve. But to suffer it is also to suffer it. Ashbery writes, "... everything is getting choked to the point of/Silence," only twelve lines after identifying "everything" as his solar source, his nearly regrettable be-all and end-all. And, three lines after that, "Suddenly all is/Loathing...," he reports. The drama of the reporting carried on in the poem responds to the narrator's sense of being doomed, overwhelmed, helpless even in midstream of his brilliant, sustaining perceptions. The claustrophobia brought on by sensory onslaught to a needfully passive observer can threaten the receiver of it. "How will it end?" asks Ashbery, only partly rhetorically, in line twenty-eight. He is forced into hysterical orality, essentially cartoonish, by the very circumstances that also afford him vitality and pleasure.

That's the first stage of the poem, exciting and monstrous, and leading logically to the appearance in line forty-three of a "borborygmic giant who even now/Is rolling over on us in his sleep." But actually, the endangering passivity of the narrator eventually allows him to recognize a fact beyond that of profusion and oppression, claustrophobia, suffering, monstrosity. As Ashbery observes in lines sixty-one to sixty-two, that fact takes form as a comment on perceptual reality: "'It's all bits and pieces, spangles, patches, really; nothing/Stands alone.'" And, forty-one lines further on, he notes, "All life is but a figment." If so, then "Not what we see but how we see it matters" (line ninety-nine). A more active player in the comic drama of the poem would not have been at liberty, ironically, to glimpse such fragmentary contingency or its innate freedoms. This fact has humorous reverberations. The whole monologue gyrates, with a bizarre, tatterdemalion imagination.

A little more about Ashbery as a stand-up comic. First, the persona that he adopts in the poem is a trademarked cartoon character known for her silly blather, woefully "female" and incognizant. The choice of persona impresses me as rather defensive on the writer's part. Ashbery is playing a game of gender tag that doubles as a critique of American mass culture. The persona keeps his attack safer, and also guards him personally. In effect, he derails cartoon commodification with the further commodification offered by a fraught poetic language, which here seeks to disturb and to own in the name of a favored consciousness: the flyaway onrush of perception and experience. This is supposed to be superior to the style of celluloid Disneyesque proliferation (and word abuse). As for the personal safeguard supplied by the persona, I think it contains odd contradictions. Ashbery feels free to "speak" via this female, and without unduly characterizing her femininity, without consenting to it as a potentially odious enveloping environment. The persona's voice sounds neutral, or male. The narrator asserts an independence from the persona that may be less than honest.

In his selection of persona, isn't Ashbery suggesting his own fear of captivity within his poems, just as Daffy Duck is a captive of the Disney industry? (See lines ten to twelve.) In other words, how can the narrator, a by-product of the poetic undertaking, escape oppression and manipulation by the poet? And, conversely, can the poet ever evade the poem as its primary subject? Would this poet like to? For that matter, can subjectivity ever be let off the hook as Ashbery's prime concern? In the best of all possible worlds, would he prefer to write about something or someone else? I doubt he has the choice. But to consider an option that isn't one might be balefully funny, and may well drive the poem.

One more thing. I haven't done justice to the impact of the poem's comic gyration, and I would like to, because this is the poem's main charm. Its sources: Ashbery's polyglot dictional range, from opera to "pix" to baking powder, is like a verbal game of Twister. (Remember that? Bodies tangled up, shaking with giggles, on a board rolled out in somebody's basement?) Even without understanding all of the diction and allusions, a reader or listener has to erupt in an inward fit of laughter before the range demonstrated. The range mimics cartoon motion and also conjures for me the punchiness of stand-up comics, who just can't stop, not even if it kills them. Then, too, there is Ashbery's perverse, highly entertaining mixture of lofty rhetoric and goofy utterance: "Wait!/ I have an announcement!" (lines thirty-seven to thirty-eight) contrasts feverishly with "I have/Only my intermittent life in your thoughts to live" (lines forty-seven to forty-eight). Likewise, "me mug's attenuated/Reflection" (lines twelve to thirteen) and "midnight micturition spree" (line thirty-four) compress high and low extremes within the short span of each phrase.

"Daffy Duck in Hollywood" leans toward the satirical in its force and its tropes. The aggressive pursuit of performance by the narrator also implies another onset of satire in the poem, as though undermining the idea that performance could represent a successful rebellion from the poet's usually more passive stance.

For these reasons, "Daffy Duck" is one of the funniest poems I've ever met. The poem is funny both for its hilarious excesses and for the underlying strains. I'm not inclined to insist on laughter as an Ashbery reader's or listener's truest response. But I do insist that Ashbery's poetry places reader and listener, at the least, in a state of witty, indulged, excoriated, full-minded repose.

## DAFFY DUCK IN HOLLYWOOD
*by John Ashbery*

Something strange is creeping across me.
La Celestina has only to warble the first few bars
Of "I Thought about You" or something mellow from
*Amadigi di Gaula* for everything—a mint-condition can
Of Rumford's Baking Powder, a celluloid earring, Speedy
Gonzales, the latest from Helen Topping Miller's fertile
Escritoire, a sheaf of suggestive pix on greige, deckle-edged
Stock—to come clattering through the rainbow trellis
Where Pistachio Avenue rams the 2300 block of Highland
Fling Terrace. He promised he'd get me out of this one,
That mean old cartoonist, but just look what he's
Done to me now! I scarce dare approach me mug's attenuated
Reflection in yon hubcap, so jaundiced, so *déconfit*
Are its lineaments—fun, no doubt, for some quack phrenologist's
Fern-clogged waiting room, but hardly what you'd call
Companionable. But everything is getting choked to the point of
Silence. Just now a magnetic storm hung in the swatch of sky
Over the Fudds' garage, reducing it—drastically—
To the aura of a plumbago-blue log cabin on
A Gadsden Purchase commemorative cover. Suddenly all is
Loathing. I don't want to go back inside any more. You meet
Enough vague people on this emerald traffic-island—no,

Not people, comings and goings, more: mutterings,
    splatterings,
The bizarrely but effectively equipped infantries of happy-
    go-nutty
Vegetal jacqueries, plumed, pointed at the little
White cardboard castle over the mill run. "Up
The lazy river, how happy we could be?"
How will it end? That geranium glow
Over Anaheim's had the riot act read to it by the
Etna-size firecracker that exploded last minute into
A *carte du Tendre* in whose lower right-hand corner
(Hard by the jock-itch sand-trap that skirts
The asparagus patch of algolagnic *nuits blanches*) Amadis
Is cozening the Princesse de Clèves into a midnight
    micturition spree
On the Tamigi with the Wallets (Walt, Blossom, and little
Skeezix) on a lamé barge "borrowed" from Ollie
Of the Movies' dread mistress of the robes. Wait!
I have an announcement! This wide, tepidly meandering,
Civilized Lethe (one can barely make out the maypoles
And *châlets de nécessité* on its sedgy shore) leads to Tophet,
    that
Landfill-haunted, not-so-residential resort from which
Some travellers return! This whole moment is the groin
Of a borborygmic giant who even now
Is rolling over on us in his sleep. Farewell bocages,
Tanneries, water-meadows. The allegory comes unsnarled
Too soon; a shower of pecky acajou harpoons is
About all there is to be noted between tornadoes. I have
Only my intermittent life in your thoughts to live

Which is like thinking in another language. Everything
Depends on whether somebody reminds you of me.
That this is a fabulation, and that those "other times"
Are in fact the silences of the soul, picked out in
Diamonds on stygian velvet, matters less than it should.
Prodigies of timing may be arranged to convince them
We live in one dimension, they in ours. While I
Abroad through all the coasts of dark destruction seek
Deliverance for us all, think in that language: its
Grammar, though tortured, offers pavilions
At each new parting of the ways. Pastel
Ambulances scoop up the quick and hie them to hospitals.
"It's all bits and pieces, spangles, patches, really; nothing
Stands alone. What happened to creative evolution?"
Sighed Aglavaine. Then to her Sélysette: "If his
Achievement is only to end up less boring than the others,
What's keeping us here? Why not leave at once?
I have to stay here while they sit in there,
Laugh, drink, have fine time. In my day
One lay under the tough green leaves,
Pretending not to notice how they bled into
The sky's aqua, the wafted-away no-color of regions supposed
Not to concern us. And so we too
Came where the others came: nights of physical endurance,
Or if, by day, our behavior was anarchically
Correct, at least by New Brutalism standards, all then
Grew taciturn by previous agreement. We were spirited
Away *en bateau*, under cover of fudge dark.
It's not the incomplete importunes, but the spookiness
Of the finished product. True, to ask less were folly, yet

If he is the result of himself, how much the better
For him we ought to be! And how little, finally,
We take this into account! Is the puckered garance satin
Of a case that once held a brace of dueling pistols our
Only acknowledging of that color? I like not this,
Methinks, yet this disappointing sequel to ourselves
Has been applauded in London and St. Petersburg. Somewhere
Ravens pray for us."
                    The storm finished brewing. And thus
She questioned all who came in at the great gate, but none
She found who ever heard of Amadis,
Nor of stern Aureng-Zebe, his first love. Some
There were to whom this mattered not a jot: since all
By definition is completeness (so
In utter darkness they reasoned), why not
Accept it as it pleases to reveal itself? As when
Low skyscrapers from lower-hanging clouds reveal
A turret there, an art-deco escarpment here, and last perhaps
The pattern that may carry the sense, but
Stays hidden in the mysteries of pagination.
Not what we see but how we see it matters; all's
Alike, the same, and we greet him who announces
The change as we would greet the change itself.
All life is but a figment; conversely, the tiny
Tome that slips from your hand is not perhaps the
Missing link in this invisible picnic whose leverage
Shrouds our sense of it. Therefore bivouac we
On this great, blond highway, unimpeded by
Veiled scruples, worn conundrums. Morning is
Impermanent. Grab sex things, swing up

Over the horizon like a boy
On a fishing expedition. No one really knows
Or cares whether this is the whole of which parts
Were vouchsafed—once—but to be ambling on's
The tradition more than the safekeeping of it. This mulch for
Play keeps them interested and busy while the big,
Vaguer stuff can decide what it wants—what maps, what
Model cities, how much waste space. Life, our
Life anyway, is between. We don't mind
Or notice any more that the sky *is* green, a parrot
One, but have our earnest where it chances on us,
Disingenuous, intrigued, inviting more,
Always invoking the echo, a summer's day.

# Barbara Guest's Drama

"THAT THERE SHOULD NEVER BE air/in a picture surprises me." The opening of Barbara Guest's poem "Roses" stays with me partly because I have been tempted, since reading more of Guest's poetry, to substitute the word "space" for "air" and "poem" for "picture."

Taking this liberty of substitution occurred to me especially after rereading "The Surface as Object." This later poem's cryptic continuities, like hieroglyphics astream in an Egyptian afterlife, become glisteningly expansive in their verbal islands as the poem's irregular visual spiral elapses.

The expansive quality of "Surface," though it contracts around the hieroglyphic islands, depends equally on the presence of clots and billows of ambient white space, a patterning element or molding medium. Guest included a coursing space here, at a later point in her writing life, although this sort of space had little place in her earlier work. The choice to include the space intrigues me. And while to assign a word like "archaic" to describe the character of "Surface" may seem inappropriate—this poem may be too free, too

Joycean, and too "modern" to absorb the adjective—still, the language and the visual form of "Surface" conjure for me an antique elation that has much to do with the poem's spatial definition.

"The Surface as Object" is far afield from the genre known as visual poetry, and I would not want to emphasize the poem's shape or physical arrangement to the detriment of its implications. For the implications embedded in the private "layered zone" of Guest's poetry confer more than a passing enigma or a personality. Rather, her private poetic zone is fundamental to the poetry. The zone is perspectival and architectural in intent and consequences, much as for a painter like de Chirico perspective proved formative— perspective as an altering, remedial, narrative means of perception and composition. For Guest, the spatial vistas of "Surface" imply inner reaches and privacies, nooks and crannies, while they also suggest outward efflux and explorations. In her case, unlike de Chirico's, space and perspective do not emerge mainly as physical issues; they are elements owned by the zone, which is mind, despite physical manifestations. But the runic withdrawal or difficulty of the zone—signifying Guest's narrative displacement from the poem, a determining displacement—is catalytic, as with de Chirico: a perspectival displacement governs the poem with an eye, even though the eye is latterly missing or retracted.

"The Surface as Object" considers what is *not* missing, what is most evident, from the perspective of one who has departed from the evidence. I enjoy the odorous ironies of the poem's occasional, playful, presumed literalisms (e.g., "jungleware") and regard them as Egyptian in flavor: as a "bittersweet grapple" with remains, in full knowledge of a recalcitrant, foretold future. Perhaps something in that grapple encourages the flourishing of a "cult-like/expressiveness" that answers in a compulsive obeisance to the grappling. I'm not sure.

But irony does not represent the poem's full intonation; instead, drama does. The drama is conveyed in part by the visual inscription of the hieroglyphic, islanded phrases and lines in Guest's space, and in part by the challenge that she seems to propose in a monologue lacking a first-person speaker. The drama, too, is perspectival, as though elicited from a series of inevitable relationships (between the portions of the poem's spiral; between the thing seen and the displaced narrator; between the Egyptian who would set out to narrate his afterlife, and the fate awaiting him).

The "gold on the guava lick of rosin" observed by Guest is as seductive as a fate can ever be, and yet the stickiness of rosin can be incidental, just a maneuvering. Taking a position in between unfamiliar or opposed perspectives, no matter how well constructed, one might pine for a larger shock, for an unexpected wildness. I am caught in the midst of Guest's runes, considering the impersonal nature of enclosure, maybe in the same way as an Egyptian might think about his tomb.

ROSES
*by Barbara Guest*

> "painting has no air..."
> —Gertrude Stein

That there should never be air
in a picture surprises me.
It would seem to be only a picture
of a certain kind, a portrait in paper
or glued, somewhere a stickiness
as opposed to a stick-to-it-ness
of another genre. It might be

quite new to do without
that air, or to find oxygen
on the landscape line
like a boat which is an object
or a shoe which never floats
and is stationary.

    Still there
are certain illnesses that require
air, lots of it. And there are nervous
people who cannot manufacture
enough air and must seek
for it when they don't have plants,
in pictures. There is the mysterious
traveling that one does outside
the cube and this takes place
in air.

    It is why one develops
an attitude toward roses picked
in the morning air, even roses
without sun shining on them.
The roses of Juan Gris from which
we learn the selflessness of roses
existing perpetually without air,
the lid being down, so to speak,
a 1912 fragrance sifting
to the left corner where we read
"The Marvelous" and escape.

*Barbara Guest's Drama*

☒

## THE SURFACE AS OBJECT
*by Barbara Guest*

the visible

as in the past

subsisting in layered zone

refuses to dangle

oaths on marsh field

whitened or planned

memorial distance

rather than vine

that which proliferates

the bittersweet grapple

initiates

a mysterious mesh

forbids   the instant disclosure

          delays a humid course

or creates a patina

         jungleware.


or she moving forward into

the line of sticks

        circled by sticks

her hand flies up

         in the direct line of sticks

odor of lines.

  knowing the difficulty

  annexation of Egypt

     oaths on marsh fields etc.


        a possible intimacy with

the tomblike fragrance of stone

       the cult-like

expressiveness.

*Barbara Guest's Drama*

(the perpendicular

millimeter stone

less raw


or, gangling

as the artful

lessening surprised.)

tree grown guava

oaths on marsh field

the hungry minstrel and the forager

gold on the guava lick of rosin

and the chill latched thicket

marsh weed

*regardez-la*

the untamed ibis.

# Short Survey of Scruples

IN SOME OF HER VERY BRIEF POEMS, Emily Dickinson is smitten by the constraints of a most demanding charge: the naming and showing of essential principles of experience and art. In this vastly exclusive yet expansive body of work, she writes as a minimalist who seeks the utmost. In the effort to abandon everything not utterly fundamental, she purges the language, reconsiders, in effect, the goals and forms of her craft, and makes strange new things possible in poetry. (They are still new now.) She scruples with the universe, and urges us into hers.

These spare poems name the essential in extremis, and they too are essential. They reveal a creed in their form, and not just by stating it. The craft of the poems is allied closely with their substance; form and content, so-called, are nearly the same thing. And the kinship leads to a paradox: the poems, though alarmingly precise in their expression, are difficult to think about, and easier to sense or feel.

Proposed as an absolute, the poetry doesn't encourage critical discussion. Instead it thrives in a realm of belief—a realm that we encounter with a severe and salutary shock. The poems are physical evidence of ethereal truth, and often refuse the distinction between the ethereal and physical. In this they are exotic; they may even seem to refuse us. Dickinson's imperiously thoughtful manner of defining the intrinsic warns us, and wards us off, with a kindling purity that won't stop. *Can you take it?* she seems to ask.

> By homely gift and hindered Words
> The human heart is told
> Of Nothing—
> "Nothing" is the force
> That renovates the World—

Where does Dickinson's authority come from in these poems? It comes, as she writes in poem 1563 (above), from "Nothing." "Nothing" is not something ambient, surrounding her. "Nothing" is her pen and first principle. "Nothing" sculpts and cuts and tests whatever is before it; it is a ruthless and divine importuner. And for Dickinson, that is most fortunate. Though this "force" of which she writes, in acclamation, "hinders" her own words, the hindrance bears down on the poet with elemental gravity. It shrivens; it extracts something—the poem—of substance and of value.

The product of so harsh a process must be fierce, and it must be mere. If "hindered" properly, the poem will pose a match, in power, for the force that coerces it. What aspects of craft contribute to the poem's power? Those that form the poem's asperity, answering to "Nothing": its iambic containment, as if chiseled by "Nothing" into alternating eight- and six-syllable lines (one bifurcated) in order to cohere; punctuation (dashes utter gasps of space and pause and possibility into the poem, as startling and physical as an onrush of "Nothing" would be to a soul); and unexpected capitalization — the daunting authorities of "Words," "Nothing," and "World" are established bodily, and in company, with their initial looming letters. The alliteration of "homely," "hindered," "human," and "heart," and of "Words" and "World," also helps to tighten a margin of containment around the bare necessities of Dickinson's World of Words. And yet, the absolution offered by "Nothing" seems, in the poem, always to be pending. In closing, the poem leaves us in a position of awaiting further word.

> There is a solitude of space
> A solitude of sea
> A solitude of death, but these
> Society shall be
> Compared with that profounder site
> That polar privacy
> A soul admitted to itself—
> Finite infinity.

Poem 1695 names a hierarchy of Nothings — ranks of "solitudes" — and proposes the most pure of all these as a prospect and a standard, absolute yet future. But the movement of this poem is different from the other's. In it Dickinson begins by collecting "solitudes" around herself in a kind of "Society," then offers a reversal, eschewing "Society" for a "polar privacy" of soul. She opts out, retreating inward, and regards the retreat as a high virtue. The privacy she chooses represents a promotion, spiritually speaking, to a solitude so hallowed it can barely be spoken of. (Two words salute it, finite and infinite in their vaulting concretion.) And the promise of the poem is an arrival in the chambers of this hallowed thing.

The poem itself has arrived; it sits in splendid privacy, surrounded on all sides by a "solitude of space," and banished from the possible sea of other words. The poem seems to meet its own death, and to affirm in good-bye. It is a token of rebellious mortality.

How does the poem rebel, and how does it arrive? By narrowing to a point. While balancing her passage with iambic lines of alternately eight and six syllables, and with expansive *s* sounds that lead later to the sharp patter of *p*'s, *t*'s, and *e*'s, Dickinson pulls down deep to a squeezed ultimate. The end of the poem imposes the only heaven possible, the only heaven imaginable to a mortal so ready to leave. That heaven feels demanded, extorting, and it feels perfect.

Take all away —
The only thing worth larceny
Is left — the Immortality —

Dickinson's brevity beatifies other poems in other ways. Poem 1365 is phrased as a demand, or perhaps as a plea. "Take all away —," the poet implores, or she exacts — and then moves on to rid, in effect, the rest of the poem of anything *but* "the only thing" needed after "all" has been taken from it. Dickinson does specify what "only thing" so distracts her: it's none other than "the Immortality." But onlyness is also something the poem takes in, glows with, shivers from.

We shun because we prize her Face
Lest sight's ineffable disgrace
Our Adoration stain

By contrast, poem 1429 is worded as though to explain or justify: "We shun because . . . ," and "lest," she writes, with the tact of a zealot. To shun something holy is an act of reverence both noted and committed by the poem; the poem seems to flinch, in conclusion, before unseen greatness. Suggests Dickinson, "Adoration" may be better felt than said, and faith will get you further without cause, proof, or fact as help.

Few, yet enough,
Enough is One—
To that ethereal throng
Have not each one of us the right
To stealthily belong?

Various poems assist her in forming a creed, but in poem 1596, Dickinson says and shows what she means with a supremely cryptic completeness. The poem is peculiar in the grandeur of its summary, even more peculiar than the others. It asks and answers the question of what, in poetry, is sufficient—what poetry can and should be.

The poem bows to unity as to a god, and yet cuts itself off from a larger unity, preferring to seize its own "stealthily." There is perversity in this approach, a brazen underhandedness, like that of a mortal person striving for godliness. The mortal well knows her own presumptuousness; she hoards it as a fuel for her maniacally honed precision. She is god's rival, a lunging spiritual entrepreneur, and it is uncertain whether, in the last judgment, the poet does good or bad, sins or transcends the sin. All we know is, she's compelled— and she compels us.

The first and most salient feature of the poem is its syntactical inversions: twice bound by this restraint, the poem would seem to submit to a higher calling. But could submission be a gesture, in part? Even bound, the poem seems to pulse, like a malcontent held under. The dogmatism of the first two lines is tossed by the query of the last three: finally not supplicant, and all aspirant, the poem sneaks in where it *doesn't* belong. Of course, it must go "stealthily."

The poem is duplicitous, and scheming to be. It salaams, and it subverts. For who is to say, after all, just how much "few" is—or how little "enough" may be? Dickinson the interloper makes measurements according to her own scale; moral specifying is the poem's action, its main cause, and the source of our rejoicing.

Yet, strangely enough, the poem is less than measured, metrically. The first line opens on a stressed syllable, drops to two that are not stressed, and rests on one that is. Although the next four lines are iambic, the syllable count is, for Dickinson, wildly irregular, with the fourth line posing an especially egregious breach: consisting of eight syllables, distributed among eight tight-lipped words, it juts out with a Puritan insistence, a defiance of decorum, moral or poetic. (The other lines are finicky, comparably.) Independence is risked, poetically—and it is championed.

The stony end-stops of the first two lines yield to two others that are resolutely enjambed, suggesting a passionate rush to join "the throng," and yet the impropriety of doing it. Spiritual conflict is structurally embedded.

And finally, what of the "One"? It is a spiritual prime number, the irreducible quantity for a believer, whether the creed be poetry, feeling, thinking, or deity. The "One" represents the authority of unity and the unity of authority, the speaking voice, the soul that writes, the "finite infinity" that knows the flavor of the infinite and yet keeps true to the narrow circle of itself.

The soul of this poet scruples, and never tires.

# Against the Gate

THERE IS A GATE JUST PAST WHERE I PAUSE. The gate is hardly visible, and I don't especially want to glimpse it. At the moment, no one is guarding the gate; it is ajar only slightly. No one is trying to barge in, because they don't realize it's ajar. A little more fanfare, a little more word, and a moil of enthusiasts would gather by the gate, trying to see across to the other side and judge for how long the gate might stay open—and whether they could pass through.

Now, despite my reluctance, *I am* spying the gate, an immaculate white wooden construction, but electronically operated (a fact at odds with its Frost-like rustic bearing), and thus a little sinister. If you can't see who is controlling the gate, its symbolism may swell—or deflate—in a morosely rhetorical manner.

This view of things suggests a bad dream, and yet it's lifelike. In life, true, the gatekeeper would probably become visible to us eventually. He (or perhaps she) could even be reached by e-mail, or failing that, through various indirect but still dependable channels— if he reads his mail. (Not all of them do.) Then, at least, the identities of the gatekeepers could gradually be verified; you could grasp what they stand for, their career biography, their claims, their accomplishments. But you could never come to know *them*, could you? And for that reason, they don't really seem to be. They are only cultural insignia. They represent an institution, literature; and every institution is oddly impervious to us.

Institutions don't belong to us, but historians and critics habitually take their measure. Historians and critics are full of their own opinions and egotisms, yet they are also supposed to find and appraise some objective truth or fact. So what would critic or historian make of the gate and its poetical keepers down the road from where I pause?

The gate and its keepers are involved too directly in literature to do any such work of appraisal. They would merely barter among themselves for a treacherous consensus. The matter of merit, besides, is just too personal for them to adjudicate. The matter of merit also merges unreliably with the issue of taste. It isn't as though taste can't ever be discussed; but the powerful stand to lose something during the discussion, and so avoid it. Would they lose the sense of pure, imperious rejoinder? The nicety of what they know? Knew? The esteemed quibble? Passion? Self-regard? How exactly could they say what they meant so that others would agree? Disagreement, dissatisfaction, can lead us downward; an anarchy is waiting there, some fatal dispute. Dispute and disagreement can topple power. And power electrifies the gate.

Power means, partly, the wish not to be surprised, and not to be toppled. But wouldn't we all be better off if our power could come instead from doubt? Wouldn't doubt be helpful in opening the landscape to each one of us?

All speculation aside, I keep thinking, in my milling, in my pause, about the geography of the gate, the picture of it.

The gate occupies such a well-known neighborhood that it easily becomes a constant point of reference in our everyday talk. The gate is a point of reference in our writing, too. Is that beneficial? Should we really remain conscious of merit and merit-seeking even as we work? Couldn't we manage a reprieve? We all must not be gatekeepers to ourselves when we write.

The gate is infirm architecture, a stopping point, a bar to the journey. Step over it, or go around it, into the woods, forgetful of merit. The gate is meant for sneaking past or slipping through. There may be no such thing as the good in poetry or ourselves.

When I look over at the gate, I can see my friends and others like them gathered in a huddle, jostling genially and gazing up at a harrowing few judges, who read and decide, at least for now. No one seems disturbed by the social estrangement. My friends lay hands on the gate, somewhat reverently, even as they joke about it, revise and consider their strategies, their stanzas. They discuss technique; the gate is dewy. They talk for hours about jobs, word choices, poetry politics, the future. The gate basks in light. Day ends, and the gaggle goes home, there to review events and ponder tomorrow.

The path is so walked, so worn. Don't we tire of it?

If you look past the way to the gate, you will learn that the woods around it are distinguished, fraught with details, a topography of the unimaginable. That's why some prefer to go there and abandon the gated way. A forest has a better mind than ours. The ground is pattered by comments and leavings, traipsing claws, breaths in the thick. Why don't we notice this?

Because we pine for the gate with its comforts, the bulwark of institutional clarity, the power, the merit, the lack of doubt. Broad

white slats, parallelism, structure, plumbness, a certain mechanism.
The lauded authority that can be leaned on, revenant of a century or
more. Do not be afraid, the gate will open for us at the right time....

And when it does, the crowd queuing nearby will shout and
careen into the close-cropped lawn beyond, a parkland for chosen
habitués. They will scatter their poems behind them, loose-
handed, happy, regardless, into the weeds they came from.

# A Questing: Adrienne Rich

ON A CITY SUBWAY, PEOPLE READ all kinds of things, from dimestore novels to the Koran. They also read poetry. For, hunched over a briefcase or a shopping bag, a rider may look up and glimpse "Delta," a short poem by Adrienne Rich, mounted on the train's inside wall as part of the Poetry Society of America's "Poetry in Motion" project. The poem can lull or challenge for as long as the trip. It is a private voice made public, and a communal link. "If you think you can grasp me, think again," the poem reads, urging an entry into some more expansive place. And it continues, "my story flows in more than one direction," as does anyone's, or could.

Poetry as a common property—as common as mass transit—is a theme dear to Rich, who deplores the hard times that have imposed shorter hours on American public libraries and the mass-market mentality that all but excludes poetry from some bookstores. She criticizes "a certain kind of by-rote presentation of poetry" as a killjoy to poems and their readers and condemns the lopsided "distribution of culture." She believes in poetry as "a questing." The questing can be made by many people in many forms, from sonnets to rap music.

In her prose work *What Is Found There: Notebooks on Poetry and Politics* (Norton, 1993), Rich considers the business, for poets, of questing, and other useful things. "The origins and nature of poetry are not just personal," she writes, convinced that poetry is innately political and an agent for change. "The question for a North American poet is how to bear witness to a reality from which the public—and maybe part of the poet—wants, or is persuaded it wants, to turn away."

Few turn away nowadays from Rich's public appearances. These are usually standing-room-only affairs attended by the faithful. Yet, sitting in her Manhattan hotel suite, the sixty-four-year-old Rich, in town during her autumn 1993 author tour, seems by manner almost modest. A southern tranquillity of syllables is surprising; her earnest affirmatives interrupt it. She smiles: small curtains seem to rise on mischievous cheeks. Dark eyes peer, warm and shrewd. The writer is physically small, and arthritis slows her now, but tenacity and dissent have made her who she is.

Not only that, but the willingness to pursue change, personal or political. "You do have to have *will* to persevere," Rich says. "You do have to have will to not give up the first time someone sends your poetry back, or the first time you stand on a street corner trying to hand out fliers, and people are tearing them up and stamping them into the mud. You have to persevere, and you also have to be willing to be alone or very few in number for a while, in order to generate anything. I'm convinced of that, even though I feel that there are so many people out there who hunger for the kinds of social connectedness that we need. I think it is important to possess a short-term pessimism and a long-term optimism — not to expect everything of any given 'campaign,' but to believe that, piece by piece, changes will come. It helps me to have lived through the '50s and the '40s as the young person I was — very apolitical, coming from a politically conservative background — and to understand all the pieces that went into my own politicization."

For Rich, poetry has always been "the place where I could have dialogues, where I could try ideas out," whether those ideas involved the urgencies of literature, leftism, feminism, or lesbian identity, to her all matters of long concern. But ironically or not, despite her habit of challenging orthodoxies, Rich began her poetic life as a formalist. "I needed those forms when I was very young," she says. "They allowed me to touch things that I wouldn't have been able to touch bare-handed. Form allowed the exploration of rather chaotic material." And though her work abandoned a formalist bent, Rich claims not to reject formalism utterly as an idea. "At best, when you're working with a form, you're [also] working against it; that creates an excitement."

In another irony, the feminist began writing at the encouragement of her father, a "very patriarchal" doctor who nevertheless introduced Rich to the work of Mary Wollstonecraft, hoping his daughter would "realize herself, while sending mixed messages about what that would mean," she says. Growing up as the child of an assimilated Jewish father and a Gentile mother in "a very southern climate in Baltimore," Rich felt "split at the root, a border person, with all of my family from the South, yet not really being of that world myself."

Her father also gave her "a wonderful gift for a child" — a rhyming dictionary. "It not only had rhymes in it, but a section showing the format for the traditional poetic forms, with examples.

It was only when I began to write as a grown woman out of the struggles of my own existence, more candidly and less formally, that he . . . 'withdrew his support' would be a mild way of putting it." Her mother, a musician, helped as well to provide "a good education for a poet."

That education gradually led her to Radcliffe College. In the same year as she graduated with honors, Rich's first book manuscript, *A Change of World* (Yale University Press, 1951), won the Yale Series of Younger Poets prize. She acknowledges, "My first two books were much praised for their technical assurance and grace," though she calls her second, *The Diamond Cutters* (1955), "that obligatory second book that no one should have to write." Harper & Row published it and also published *Snapshots of a Daughter-in-Law* (1963), a book in which a new question was "pressing itself to the fore: 'What does it mean to be a woman and a poet?'"

Married in 1953 to Alfred Haskell Conrad, an economist, Rich had had "three children in rapid succession" and soon found that she was "hardly reading, being tired a great deal, and writing, when I did write, only very brief poems." She explains, "I was a well-brought-up and fairly protected young woman who was often torn between what I experienced as my desire and what I thought I had to do to be a 'real woman,' or acceptable. So a lot of the poems in *Snapshots* were showing the stress marks of those tensions. In those years, my quest was also to understand the world in larger terms than personal life, to get a bigger picture."

She was aided in that quest by her reading of James Baldwin, Simone de Beauvoir, and Martin Luther King, Jr. "De Beauvoir's *The Second Sex* was a gift to me at the end of the '50s, because I saw that there was a larger context in which my struggles to understand myself in the world as a woman could be integrated . . . and I could make that into poetry." Rich began "truly probing in a poem, 'Is this what I want to say, or is this what Poetry, with a capital 'P,' has taught me is what should be said?' I think that is an important kind of interior question for young poets, and for all poets, to keep asking. Tradition is important, but the voices of tradition can, in your head, become other people's voices that you're using instead of your own."

When she broke with formalism and began writing free verse, Rich was encouraged by her discovery of poets Denise Levertov, Charles Olson, and William Carlos Williams. Levertov, who became a friend, was especially influential. "A lot of the poets of my generation had been hit by this dictum of Robert Frost's that writing free verse is like playing tennis with the net down—a very disparaging dictum." Instead, Rich and others found that free verse "was as exacting an art as formalism, and it felt much more risky. Free verse was so demanding, from line to line, and from pause to pause, and from breath to breath.

"The poet Muriel Rukeyser said—and I agree with her—that we must think of a poem as a transfer of energy. Energy within the poet goes into the poem, but then must go from the poem to a reader or a listener. There has to be this transfer of energy. And how is that going to come about except through the way that the words are used in the poem, the way they are framed, the way they are poised, the torque?"

However, sometimes the transfer is intercepted or disturbed. For example, *Snapshots of a Daughter-in-Law* was "attacked," Rich calmly notes. "With that book, in which I began to break open forms and write more as a woman, I found that the critics were not so pleased with me anymore. I was told that I had become bitter and personal. The word 'political' wasn't being used then, but it would be later, as a pejorative. There was hostility out there to examination of the very issues that were most crucial to me." In addition, her tenure with Harper turned out to be a mixed blessing. "Their last poet had been Edna St. Vincent Millay, and what they basically wanted to know was: was I going to sell like she had?"

Levertov, then advising Norton on its poetry series, recommended Rich's work, with the result that *Necessities of Life*, her next book of poetry, was published by Norton in 1966. Since then, she has remained with the house, publishing more than a dozen books of award-winning poetry and prose. Until his death, her editor was for many years John Benedict.

What accounts for such a long-standing publishing relationship? "I remember getting a letter from John telling me how he felt about *The Will to Change* [1971]," she replies. "It was like no other letter I had gotten. The letter was full of empathy for my work and excitement about the direction it was taking. It wasn't the kind of letter that said, 'Well, we really loved what you did in your last two books, and we hope you will be doing more of the same.' It was saying, 'I can't wait to see what you do next.' We had our ups and downs, of course, but with John, there was never any sense of having to contend over what I was writing. He was there with it, though sometimes it made him very uneasy." For instance, "he scribbled questions all over the manuscript of *Of Woman Born* [1976] that betokened certain anxieties—anxieties of a man threatened and yet, in some way, attracted by changing senses of what was possible in terms of gender. But I was absolutely free to publish that book as I saw fit. And certainly that was always true of the poetry."

Unlike many poets, Rich has also written a good deal of prose on various subjects, collected in several books besides *What Is Found*

*There.* "I started writing prose because, as a poet, I was occasionally asked to write book reviews. The first published prose that I wrote was some reviews for *Poetry* magazine back in the mid-'60s. Then, as the '60s began to intensify politically, and as I became much more politically involved, living in New York and teaching on the Columbia and CCNY campuses in '68 and '69, and beginning to understand my world, both the personal and the larger, in more political terms, I also found myself in the situation of writing things like fliers and press releases and ad hoc documents. And then, as the women's movement began to crest, I began to be asked to speak, and to contribute essays to this or that publication, and I began to find that I loved writing prose, which was not something I'd ever felt I could do. One of the reasons I had not felt I could write prose was that it would have been almost appalling to me to set forth in prose the kinds of things I was trying to deal with in poetry until there was a [public] context [for it]. People seemed to take poetry much less seriously than prose. Prose would have seemed much more self-exposing."

But exposure is part of the transfer of energy that Rukeyser intended, whether brought about in sentences or stanzas, on the page or on the subway. And it seems unlikely that Rich or her readers would really regard her "exposures" as anything less than absolutely required.

DELTA
*by Adrienne Rich*


If you have taken this rubble for my past
raking through it for fragments you could sell

know that I long ago moved on
deeper into the heart of the matter

If you think you can grasp me, think again:
my story flows in more than one direction
a delta springing from the riverbed
with its five fingers spread

☒

SNAPSHOTS OF A DAUGHTER-IN-LAW
*by Adrienne Rich*

1.
You, once a belle in Shreveport,
with henna-colored hair, skin like a peachbud,
still have your dresses copied from that time,
and play a Chopin prelude
called by Cortot: *"Delicious recollections*
*float like perfume through the memory."*

Your mind now, mouldering like wedding-cake,
heavy with useless experience, rich
with suspicion, rumor, fantasy,
crumbling to pieces under the knife-edge
of mere fact. In the prime of your life.

Nervy, glowering, your daughter
wipes the teaspoons, grows another way.

# A Questing: Adrienne Rich

2.

Banging the coffee-pot into the sink
she hears the angels chiding, and looks out
past the raked gardens to the sloppy sky.
Only a week since They said: *Have no patience.*

The next time it was: *Be insatiable.*
Then: *Save yourself; others you cannot save.*
Sometimes she's let the tapstream scald her arm,
a match burn to her thumbnail,

or held her hand above the kettle's snout
right in the woolly steam. They are probably angels,
since nothing hurts her any more, except
each morning's grit blowing into her eyes.

3.

A thinking woman sleeps with monsters.
The beak that grips her, she becomes. And Nature,
that sprung-lidded, still commodious
steamer-trunk of *tempora* and *mores*
gets stuffed with it all:       the mildewed orange-flowers,
the female pills, the terrible breasts
of Boadicca beneath flat foxes' heads and orchids.

Two handsome women, gripped in argument,
each proud, acute, subtle, I hear scream
across the cut glass and majolica
like Furies cornered from their prey:
The argument *ad feminam,* all the old knives

that have rusted in my back, I drive in yours,
*ma semblable, ma soeur!*

4.
Knowing themselves too well in one another:
their gifts no pure fruition, but a thorn,
the prick filed sharp against a hint of scorn . . .
Reading while waiting
for the iron to heat,
writing, *My Life had stood—a Loaded Gun—*
in that Amherst pantry while the jellies boil and scum,
or, more often,
iron-eyed and beaked and purposed as a bird,
dusting everything on the whatnot every day of life.

5.
*Dulce ridens, dulce loquens,*
she shaves her legs until they gleam
like petrified mammoth-tusk.

6.
When to her lute Corinna sings
neither words nor music are her own;
only the long hair dipping
over her cheek, only the song
of silk against her knees
and these
adjusted in reflections of an eye.

Poised, trembling and unsatisfied, before
an unlocked door, that cage of cages,
tell us, you bird, you tragical machine—
is this *fertilisante douleur?* Pinned down
by love, for you the only natural action,
are you edged more keen
to prise the secrets of the vault? has Nature shown
her household books to you, daughter-in-law,
that her sons never saw?


7.
*"To have in this uncertain world some stay*
*which cannot be undermined, is*
*of the utmost consequence."*
                                        Thus wrote
a woman, partly brave and partly good,
who fought with what she partly understood.
Few men about her would or could do more,
hence she was labelled harpy, shrew and whore.


8.
"You all die at fifteen," said Diderot,
and turn part legend, part convention.
Still, eyes inaccurately dream
behind closed windows blankening with steam.
Deliciously, all that we might have been,
all that we were—fire, tears,
wit, taste, martyred ambition—

stirs like the memory of refused adultery
the drained and flagging bosom of our middle years.

9.
*Not that it is done well, but*
*that it is done at all?* Yes, think
of the odds! or shrug them off forever.
This luxury of the precocious child,
Time's precious chronic invalid, —
would we, darlings, resign it if we could?
Our blight has been our sinecure:
mere talent was enough for us —
glitter in fragments and rough drafts.

Sigh no more, ladies.
                      Time is male
and in his cups drinks to the fair.
Bemused by gallantry, we hear
our mediocrities over-praised,
indolence read as abnegation,
slattern thought styled intuition,
every lapse forgiven, our crime
only to cast too bold a shadow
or smash the mould straight off.

For that, solitary confinement,
tear gas, attrition shelling.
Few applicants for that honor.

10.                              Well,
she's long about her coming, who must be
more merciless to herself than history.
Her mind full to the wind, I see her plunge
breasted and glancing through the currents,
taking the light upon her
at least as beautiful as any boy
or helicopter,

                    poised, still coming,
her fine blades making the air wince
but her cargo
no promise then:
delivered
palpable
ours.

# Waste Lands

WHY DO POETRY READINGS TEND sometimes to bring out the monotone in poets' voices? Writing isn't drudgery, and reading isn't. Performance shouldn't be. Hearing poetry read aloud or recited from memory ought to heighten our sense of the poetic, not numb it or dull our minds to slump and doze. More often than is necessary, though, attacks of institutionitis seem to overwhelm performers of poems in midstream, if not at the very start. Then they lose all their motive and become mysteriously stoic. They may even mumble. The poems fade. I yawn like a fool, wondering why they wrote at all.

In our era of the spoken word, when Sharon Stone willingly intones Emily Dickinson's poetry on audiocassette, and when "Selected Shorts" programs in New York draw enthusiastic crowds to Symphony Space, it may seem ungracious to criticize the style of poetry readings. We really do have a lot to choose from, after all: poets of the ear often perform with the musical force of singers, and actors and actresses can restore theatrical values to literature. In between these two poles of performance are found a variety of other approaches, from that of the egoless poet who is barely present during her reading to another who gossips before and after singing each of his poems.

Even so, many poetry readings remain threateningly precious or lifeless. This isn't because a quiet manner in a poet must be inherently limiting. The poet Elizabeth Macklin's audience, for example, will quickly appreciate her startling poise and musical nuances even though her voice sounds rather like an enriched whisper, resonantly delicate. The drama of restraint is not small, especially when she is paired with a folksy or boisterous sensibility in the poetry she has chosen to read—Frank O'Hara's, for instance. Likewise, the unassuming reading manner of Jorie Graham leaves an impression. Plain-spoken, elastic, and self-forgetful, her voice presents the poetry straightforwardly and well. By contrast, the rich, unguent vocalism of Yusef Komunyakaa suggests jazz and blues in a lyric wash vaguely reminiscent of Dylan Thomas. Charles Bernstein's antic verbal gusto—his Manhattan mouthiness—bounces and billows. And Adrienne Rich's voice carries her unadorned dignity to us with an authority that seems remarkably pure.

How much further taste could venture where poetry performance is concerned was clarified for me in 1996 when the British actress Fiona Shaw, making her American theatrical debut, performed a staged reading of T. S. Eliot's *The Waste Land* at New York City's Liberty Theater. Never having seen Shaw act before, I had no idea what to expect from the poem I had once memorized. I was left all the less prepared for Shaw's dramatic immolation of Eliot by another *Waste Land* production I had seen a few weeks earlier in Chicago.

The Chicago *Waste Land*, directed by Bernard Sahlins and

starring Nicholas Rudall, combined musical interludes (most prevalently, Stravinsky's *The Rite of Spring*) with slide projections of artwork, evoking scenes and states of mind from the poem while it was performed. The three-person cast included two women in addition to Rudall, seen in a series of tableaux punctuated neatly by blackouts. Though tasteful and true to the poem's sources and the poet's influences, the Chicago *Waste Land* was a largely respectful historical reconstruction: literal-minded, accessible, obeisant. Watching it was like doing time in the comfortable chambers of a big American museum. The museumy feeling also had something to do with the site of the Chicago *Waste Land*: an innocuous auditorium in one of Northwestern University's modern downtown office buildings.

By contrast, the *Waste Land* that arrived in New York from England, starring Shaw and directed by Deborah Warner, was staged in the bedraggled crypt of the Liberty Theater on West 42nd Street. Built in 1904, the theater was closed in 1990, and felt to me far more abandoned than that vintage would indicate—you expected to see a charred starlet rising phoenixlike on your left. The perfume of the past, like the scent of regret, was a compelling theatrical ingredient, although the seats were far from plush, and the chilly air of the theater seemed to settle you somewhere in between two kinds of consciousness. When Shaw appeared after a churchy wait, there was no fanfare and no pretense. But we all, I think, sensed a change of light and of costive intelligence.

Hers was the stormiest nuanced solo I have ever seen, virtuosic for her lunges from one kind of voice (and emotion) to another. Shaw both revived the poem and made it seem unfamiliar, as though she were reimagining it from the beginning, and doing so once only. The performance was singular. It had nothing in common with most poetry performances. It seemed meant to do damage. Shaw's vocal range hit working-class Cockney and the Brahmin excelsior; states of tacky doom; robustly bawdy humor; eviscerated spirit; childlike insouciance. I suppose you could say that her imagination reminded me of Eliot's, on rather different expressive terms, although she never impersonated his own reading style or embodied his known social or moral proprieties.

Eliot's naysayers have lately regarded him as cold, bigoted, and dry, unfriendly to humanity. Maybe so. But I have always felt suspicious of this partial view. He also seems like someone who must have disciplined and martyred himself to his feelings by restraining and transmuting them to a grievous degree. How else to account for the cramped depth of emotional experience observed indirectly in the poetry?

The poet and critic Randall Jarrell planned to write a book about the psychology of Eliot's work. Although he never wrote it, in 1962 Jarrell gave a talk at the first National Poetry Festival in Washington, D.C., entitled "Fifty Years of American Poetry." His remarks included these about Eliot:

> Surely you must have seen that he was one of the most
> subjective and daemonic poets who ever lived, the
> victim and helpless beneficiary of his own inexorable
> compulsions, obsessions?... But... after the first few
> years, his poetry existed undersea, thousands of feet
> below that deluge of exegesis, explication, source listing,
> scholarship, and criticism that overwhelmed it. And yet
> how bravely and personally it survived... full of human
> anguish!

This was the Eliot that Shaw evoked.

Not all poets can be great actors when reading their poems to us. But plenty could do better than they have done. Take a leaf from Shaw's book.

# The Poetry of Paucity

As EVERYONE SEEMS TO KNOW, *The English Patient* is a large and glamorous film, adapted and directed by Anthony Minghella from the novel by Michael Ondaatje, about obsession and betrayal — personal, fraternal, amatory, historic, international. These two engulfing themes of the movie, however, are helpfully honed and defined by a principle of paucity. Although the scope of the movie threatens at times to slip into melodrama, urged along by a magnificent North African desert dreamscape setting, and by the absolving magnifications of frenzied wartime, happily the slip is not completed.

The sprawl of the film, like the sprawl of the desert, is cathartic: something to gaze on and smart from. Yet the ample scale of *The English Patient* isn't the reason why the movie's obsessions and betrayals travel to us eloquently. Rather, forces of compression, suppression, and reduction in visual composition and narrative style help to convey emotion, made dramatic and seductive by reluctance of means, by indirection, constriction, and by a guarded manner. That's paucity. The film's emotion is largely one of being wounded (with the wound hoarded), felt by a main cast of five (Almásy, Mrs. Clifton, Hana, Kip, Caravaggio) and by their subordinates and sidekicks. If we knew any more about the five and their wounds, there would be less emotion to go around, oddly. Wounds may demand disguises, sleights, ellipses, and opacity to dress and present their potency, and to prepare us for them.

Evidence of the movie's taste for paucity? Nobody's past, no matter how pertinent, is explained. Almásy, the Hungarian count who obsessively searches the desert for artifacts, simply refuses to tell Mrs. Clifton, his English colleague and eventual inamorata, why he has come to be there in the first place, surrounded by a tidal extinction of sand. But the sand suggests part of his answer, as any metaphor can; it piles up substance as a kind of absence, veiling deep cuts in the earth's rockery and in evolutionary human culture. The sand can bury memory and responsibility, exposing the present in extremity by annihilating all that has preceded it, and offering freedom.

More mundanely, the camera eye in the film is obligingly — even ruthlessly — editorial, omitting so many possible views of places and people that what survive, selected sedulously, are stark essentials: the proprietary, civilized nose of an exemplary British explorer, exhibited as he does his duty unambiguously. The fawnlike, baffled cruelty of a Muslim nurse who is about to torture a political prisoner, innocently, at the insistence of a German soldier. Mrs. Clifton's noble brow and Almásy's slightly simian one, equally attractive and equally helpless in the brain. The intensity of mounting emotional complications in the film feels as if extracted from an imagery of encompassing dryness. Little else remains but crystallized and flammable emotions, ready to go the way of smoke in an evaporating landscape.

Each time I have seen *The English Patient*, it comes as a relief and a consolation to me, as though I am rereading something that I need badly. The movie confirms woundedness as a possibly redemptive condition after a betrayal, offering some reprieve, and confirms woundedness as a useful guide to telling a story at cost, in the right way. The telling, too, is meant to wound, and should be. In the film's urgency to compress, suppress, and reduce, more seems to be revealed, and with it our desire for more still has got to grow. This is almost as if, having been betrayed and wounded, one could then imagine deprivation more fully than before, and also could better resist it.

According to such a logic, anyone's life may be like a series of thefts—or evaporations; your personal stock of material is gradually taken from you in incident after incident, until you are left incrementally angry or bereaved. It is next up to you to choose how to respond: with recriminatory action (by committing a betrayal or a robbery of your own) or with a philosophical murmur, by way of reaction.

Telling is the hardest thing to do after a betrayal or a wounding, and so the philosophical murmur, muted though it tends to sound, may be more heroic than any likely action. The difficulty, however, lies in knowing how to tell about betrayal, the wound perhaps most lasting.

In the movie, the predatory hero, Almásy, is best known for his ability to speak many languages and for his preference for talking only rarely and sparely. After doing his share of damage (the consequences of his betrayals include deaths, atrocities, and an enormous emotional surcharge), he is dying from war injuries very slowly in a nurse's care, at the age of thirty-something, less able to talk—though with more to tell—than ever before. Talking endangers his dwindling health and stamina, yet he must do it, for at last he has a listener, some leisure, and death coming on. Still, he feels he can't talk because he can't allow himself to remember his past, with all of his betrayals—this, more than other hurts, seems to impose too great a wound on him. All the same, he survives for just long enough to remember and to tell. Such a fate all but justifies his betrayals and himself.

But any synopsis is likely to tell little. Imagery can be more telling. The way Ralph Fiennes, for example, playing Almásy, opened his mouth during his dangerous desert heyday, when adultery with Mrs. Clifton had begun to harrow a normally cynical, well-immunized mind, is an image that stays with me. He opened his mouth wider than necessary before he took a drink, with an unconscious savoring of risk. He showed pride in the pause before the swallow, and in the nothing that was said. Much later, when he wept, his mouth opened wider and wider and wider, surprised and surprising, almost totalitarian in natural magnitude. These moments were at odds with the character's more typical discretion, contempt, silence, and manner of hunting down what he wanted.

Opening his mouth was what made him human; closing it kept him predatory. But to open an oft-closed mouth makes it look especially mammoth, like an organ of eloquence and grandeur, even when (notably when) no words are being uttered. Paucity can goad and serve feeling, though this may be a secret not commonly shared.

# Oopalie Operajita

WE DON'T BELIEVE IN GODS, yet we do believe in artists, possibly to our distinct disadvantage. How very odd of us this is. It might be better to believe in both. But can we do it, now? That's what I was wondering when I was watching Oopalie Operajita dance. She was embodying the vision of a poet, Jayadeva, who had written songs and verse while beguiled long ago by another dancer. Everyone's preoccupation—theirs, ours—was love, the then of it and the now entwined so ripely that a bystander must be overwhelmed, as if swooning. Before this none of us can be skeptics anymore. Those crafty, curling undulations of her wrist; the never-ending rotation of her hips, like a gerund allowed to become and become, turning in a lengthy sentence; that entranced articulation of fingers as an effulgence or a flowering—the description seems somehow too pedigreed, and more manneristic than the dancing. Such are the vices of a godless writer. But please remember: Operajita *is* a lyric poem, a figure of erotic dignity and tunefulness.

99

In her book *Snakes and Ladders* (Doubleday, 1997), Gita Mehta has written about India that "art is not just something displayed by the talented to a passive audience but, rather, that moment when the artist, the audience, the subject, the discipline — all combine to become something approaching religious experience, a moment of mutual creation." A reader must become part of a poem, much as Jayadeva became part of the dance that inspired his writing. He was said to write while he watched his dancer, his beloved. Perhaps as a consequence, the *Gita Govinda,* Jayadeva's classic poem of twelfth-century Orissa, tells of the love of a mythic twosome, Krishna and Radha. Back to Mehta: "Jayadeva sang of the milkmaid Radha's adoration for a beautiful young cowherd with a dark complexion and a perfect body, who plays haunting music on his flute and seduces every milkmaid, breaking Radha's heart even as he increases the intensity of her desire. The cowherd is the divine Krishna." Since he is a god, and not just a cowherd, the *Gita Govinda* is understood to be "an allegory of the human soul's love for God," according to Barbara Stoler Miller, who has translated the *Gita Govinda* from Sanskrit into English.

The poem has been closely linked with dance from the start, lending itself to various musical renditions and traditions across India. One of those who has paid homage to the Krishna-Radha tale is Guru Kelucharan Mohapatra, a renowned teacher and choreographer of Odissi, one of India's long-lasting forms of dance. The guru is thought to have outdone himself with a solo piece, "Kuru Yadu Nandana," that asks a dancer, in portraying Radha, to play the orchestra of her face and body with uncanny emotional and physical musicianship. To Western eyes, she seems both an actress and a dancer. This spectacle of intimate, prolonged exposure relies for fulfillment on the complexities of gesture, an essential aspect of Indian dance. As luck would have it, the solo was performed in 1996 by Oopalie Operajita at New York City's Symphony Space, under the auspices of the World Music Institute, as part of Kelucharan Mohapatra's seventieth birthday celebration. He is her guru, and he was present.

The dance and its performance were startling and instructive for anyone interested in touch, including poets. The effect of Odissi's array of elaborated gestural choices is to invoke the act of touching and being touched in lambent detail as a criterion for art and experience. A commonplace Odissi dancer will seem to be a chronic code-guzzler, ecstatically aping the gestural script she has inherited. But a virtuoso will do something else, almost unhoped for, and almost insane: she'll remind us that every moment is a making.

How does she do it? (Yes, she—for Indian classical dance tends to be dominated by women.) Not only with her face but also with her arms, her hips, and especially her hands, all of them undergoing a miragelike transformation by force of musical impulse. The impulse completes itself in a series of intricate curved shapes, a very slow and subtle rippling, until even a pinky finger looks seriously radial, as though it had never once been (or could ever be) peninsular or static. The coagulant draftsmanship of dance and dancer evokes manifold softnesses, until the entire stage seems taken up with touching, although it is occupied by just one woman. Gradual and bedizening as the experience of watching her may be— the dancer's conjured emotions seem to line up and preen along her like jewels or plumes—despite this, her style is unmincingly assertive. You never quite forget, in the languor of the dream, that the dancer is trying to confide something to you. And there is nearly too much to confide, an excess of intimacy.

When she dances as Radha in love with Krishna, following the story suggested in the lyric poetry of the *Gita Govinda,* does a dancer do the work of depiction or incarnation? Either one—it's up to her guru and to her. Oopalie Operajita did both, giving her performance a lifelike fullness that impressed me as realistic and recklessly romantic at the same time. Poetry can do something similar, though not all poetry wants to; Walt Whitman did it in the record of life he drew and also in the rapture he gave back to the life by writing of it. Oopalie Operajita's inclination to describe and define feelings in her dancing, while also letting the feelings well over and define her, gave a poignant fineness to the making of those moments in her performance—a quality of never ending, even when the moments ended. She seemed to be saying, this making can continue and continue, like a sort of touch. Perhaps that is what she most wanted.

A poem is often made in the mind, not in public. And poetry is not always intrinsically a performance in the way that almost any dance must be. For that reason, we can forget how nearly tangible—how like a touch—is a poem's making.

Oopalie Operajita prolonged the touch she had begun, as if remembering a god who had been touching her. She was being reminded of the god's touch, and was fulfilling that touch in turn. The first to receive her touch was Krishna, implied though not onstage beside her. Then the touch eventually came round to fall on us, the audience. This is how a dancer can make a moment.

# The Subject of a Poem Is Astonishment: Charles Simic

CHARLES SIMIC IS YUGOSLAV AND AMERICAN, skeptic and believer, a poet convinced, as he once wrote, that "writing is always a rough translation from wordlessness into words." Poetry "attracts me because it makes trouble for thinkers," he has declared. "Poetry is an orphan of silence. The words never quite equal the experience behind them. We are always at the beginning, eternal apprentices, thrown back again and again into that condition."

In his collection *The Book of Gods and Devils* (Harcourt Brace Jovanovich, 1990), Simic returned to a beginning of another kind: his early years (1958 to 1961) in New York City. In "The Initiate" he writes, "In that whole city you could hear a pin drop./Believe me,/I thought I heard a pin drop and I went looking for it." The poetry's locales are 14th Street, Hell's Kitchen, and the old Fourth Avenue booksellers' row, where readers find the figure of a young man pursuing "the great secret which kept eluding me:/knowing who I am."

Recalls Simic, "I came to New York in August of 1958, and it was amazingly simple. I would work at some place for a few months, and quit. I'd live the life of a bohemian. Then I'd realize I was running out of money, and I'd get a haircut—and a new job. I had all sorts of office jobs. I got to be pretty good at bookkeeping. I went to school at NYU; it took me ten years to get a B.A. at night. All that seemed perfectly fine. It was great to be in New York and have a job and buy records and go to movies and jazz clubs. All those street scenes, sights, made a tremendous impression on my mind—I have an endless anthology of them.

"I was aware, in writing *The Book of Gods and Devils*, of an almost pagan impulse," he continues. "Pagans would invent gods or demons for any place where people had had intense experiences. A big city is a home of multiple gods, not just the obvious religions. There are things one worships and things one is afraid of. I have a certain pessimism about history that is very Balkan; I'm suspicious of attempts to idealize human beings. We are not noble savages, not kind, good, wholesome. But I don't think the demons are very strong in the book; there is a lot of humor, and there are a lot of gods."

What he calls "the shock" of New York helped make Simic what he is. So did his solitude there. As his poem "The Immortal" tells it, "You had your own heartbeat to listen to./You were perfectly alone and anonymous./It would have taken months for anyone/To begin to miss you."

He elaborates, sitting at the dining room table of his house in Strafford, New Hampshire. "You're lonely, you're figuring out everything from scratch. You're broke. I used to spend evenings on long walks, looking at store windows, watching people. But it was a great feeling. I drifted in the most pleasant fashion. It was a time of purity. Cities are places of sphinxes, enigmas. Even though you may think about them for the rest of your life, you'll never come to the bottom of it. You're the sum of everything you don't understand."

A tall, pale, and exuberant man, Simic has lived with his wife Helen for many years in the New Hampshire woods and admits happily to his "peasant" heritage, but his relish for things urban is vigorously evident when he says, "You could smell a certain lunacy in New York. And there's always been an element of the grotesque in my work; much in *The Book of Gods and Devils* seems totally surrealist. Yet it's based on the most factual stuff imaginable." Moreover, he argues, he is "a realist and a surrealist, always drawn between the two." By way of example, he invokes "The Fourteenth Street Poem," set in "a long block/Favored by doomsday prophets," where an obstreperous bag lady holds court. It is "real," but to a heightened degree.

As he confides in a rumblingly resonant voice, "There is a story to this lady." Simic doesn't just talk—he groans, whoops, and whispers, offering heavily accented phrases that slide and twist with American slang.

"The first time I saw her, I was crossing Washington Square Park late one night. This woman of uncertain age comes up to me, with flying hair. And she says to me, 'I'm Venus, the goddess of love. If you don't give me a dollar, I'm gonna curse you, and you'll be unhappy in love.'" Simic laughs ringingly and uproariously at the absurdity of his predicament. "So I said to her, 'Beat it!' And I told myself, 'I'm cursed. There's nothing I can do.'

"A couple of months went by. I was at Barnes & Noble. It's late afternoon, I'm getting some book, I look up and there she is! So I just sort of blurt out, 'You're Venus, the goddess of love!' And she says, 'How did you *know?*'"

Being a raw youth in *echt* New York thus had its charm. "I was ignorant, and I'm glad now that I was," Simic says. "A lot of it came from being an immigrant and having really, really low expectations."

He regards his early life and world wanderings with a certain dark merriment. "My travel agents were Hitler and Stalin. They were the reason I ended up in the United States." Born in Yugoslavia in 1938, he survived the World War II bombing of Belgrade, where his family lived and his father worked as a telephone engineer for a branch office of Western Electric. In 1944 his father was captured by the Germans, who examined the blueprints in his suitcase—intended for installing phone service in mountain villages—and judged them highly suspicious. "It looked pretty bad for him—it looked like they were going to shoot him. But he was liberated by the Americans and went to Trieste." Simic and his mother meanwhile made several attempts to cross the Yugoslav border into Austria; in 1953 they were finally permitted to immigrate legally. Before joining the elder Simic in the United States, where he was again working as an engineer, they spent a year or so in Paris.

Simic, precociously on the outs with adult authorities, found himself in trouble with French schoolmasters. "I knew I was doomed. I was gonna pump gas on some turnpike outside of Paris." But in 1954 the family was reunited, and he landed in New York "speechless with excitement." The Simics soon proceeded to Chicago, where his father had been transferred; he went to the same Oak Park high school that had claimed Ernest Hemingway as a student. "When I finished high school, I was so happy! All my sins had been absolved." A great, guttural laugh shakes him.

Insists Simic, "I don't feel in any way Yugoslavian," though he has visited the East Bloc before and since its democratization.

"Sometimes this comes to me with some regret. But the first literature I knew was American literature. Most of the important things in my life happened to me in this country. There's no question that many of my outlooks are completely Slavic: Hitler and Stalin fought over my soul, my destiny. Yet I'm never classified among the exiled writers. I really could not go back now. I see things differently. And the language you write in, you have to hear."

Actually, Simic was a painter first, not a poet. In his essay collection *Wonderful Words, Silent Truth* (University of Michigan Press, 1990), he writes, "One day, two of my friends confessed that they wrote poetry. I asked them to show it to me. I wasn't impressed with what I saw. I went home and wrote some poems myself, in order to demonstrate to them how it's supposed to be done. At first, the act of writing and the initial impression were exhilarating. Then, to my astonishment, I realized that my poems were as stupid as theirs were. I couldn't figure it out... [but] in the process of writing, I discovered a part of myself, an imagination and a need to articulate certain things, that I could not afterwards forget."

His first published poems appeared in the winter 1959 issue of the *Chicago Review*. Simic enthusiastically accepted many influences: Edgar Lee Masters, Vachel Lindsay, Ezra Pound, Walt Whitman, Hart Crane. But while serving in the U.S. Army in 1962, he destroyed his work to date and started over again. As he explained in a 1972 interview, "When confronted with the life I was leading at the time, [I was impressed by the poems as] no more than literary vomit... Life and its intensity had conquered."

The literary struggle that followed was difficult and prolonged. The results led Simic to join "a generation of writers who are committed to experimentalism, so much so that I'm struck by the timidity and predictability of a lot of writing today. I read books and get mad. In American poetry at the moment, 75 percent of American experience is invisible." Simic's first book, *What the Grass Says*, was published by Kayak Press in 1967. "It had a tremendous circulation—something like twenty-seven reviews," he recalls, and was followed by *Somewhere Among Us a Stone Is Taking Notes*, also a Kayak release.

His success as a poet meant that Simic, by then married and living in New York still, received invitations from universities to teach. "Incredible! How could that be? But little by little I realized that working two days a week is better than working five." He is now a professor of English at the University of New Hampshire. "I could live and die in a good library," he has written. Yet, "I'm suspicious of the pedantry that kind of learning is prone to." He confesses to a horror of abstractions and the intellectuals that go with them. Too many of the latter, he feels, have disgraced themselves as collaborators in corrupt regimes of one kind or another to retain much credibility as a group.

Poems from Simic's first two books, along with new ones, were published by George Braziller in *Dismantling the Silence* in 1971. Braziller was Simic's main publisher for fifteen years, issuing six books that included Simic's *Selected Poems* (1985). The poet has also translated more than half a dozen volumes of poetry, among these the work of Ivan Lalic, Vasko Popa ("an enormous influence on me"), and Tomaz Salamun. "In order to do a translation, you have to be a kind of shaman—you have to pretend, for a moment, that you're somebody else. You realize that the other person is very different from you, *disgustingly* different. That's fascinating."

In 1986, Harcourt Brace Jovanovich became Simic's publisher.

"I had a good friend at HBJ, Drenka Willen, who was interested in me. George [Braziller] had always been very nice. But then you sort of say, would I be happy someplace else?" Simic decided he could be after receiving a Pulitzer prize for poetry for *The World Doesn't End*, a collection of prose poems.

"*The World Doesn't End* happened without too much deliberation," Simic maintains, marveling at winning the Pulitzer "lottery." What did the prose poem form offer him that poetry had not? "A lyric impulse is an impulse in which everything stands still," he replies. "It's like a song that repeats. Nothing ever happens in a lyric poem. It's a great acknowledgment of the present moment. In a prose sentence, however, things do happen. A prose poem is a dialectic between the two. You write in sentences, and tell a story, but the piece is like a poem because it circles back on itself.

"Books of poems — it takes a long time for the writer to really understand what's inside them," he admits. "It's like being in a period of your life." Simic reflects on the version of himself that appears in *The Book of Gods and Devils*. "It's amusing to see oneself at that distance. It isn't personal anymore. As you get older, the subject of a poem is astonishment at what is before you. It's almost a religious experience, one of standing apart and seeing yourself in awe before the world."

PARADISE
*by Charles Simic*

In a neighborhood once called "Hell's Kitchen"
Where a beggar claimed to be playing Nero's fiddle
While the city burned in mid-summer heat;
Where a lady barber who called herself Cleopatra

Wielded the scissors of fate over my head
Threatening to cut off my ears and nose;
Where a man and a woman went walking naked
In one of the dark side streets at dawn.

I must be dreaming, I told myself.
It was like meeting a couple of sphinxes.
I expected them to have wings, bodies of lions:
Him with his wildly tattooed chest;
Her with her huge, dangling breasts.

It happened so quickly, and so long ago!

You know that time just before the day breaks
When one yearns to lie down on cool sheets
In a room with shades drawn?
The hour when the beautiful suicides
Lying side by side in the morgue
Get up and walk out into the first night.

The curtains of cheap hotels flying out of windows
Like sea gulls, but everything else quiet . . .
Steam rising out of the subway gratings . . .
Bodies glistening with sweat . . .
Madness, and you might even say, paradise!

# The Cost of Poetry

"THERE'S NO MONEY IN POETRY," Robert Graves once wrote, "but then there's no poetry in money either."

I had always assumed money was a taboo subject in discussing poetry. But to think about money and poetry together tends to lower our standard of idealism to a level that is useful: poetry isn't expected to be profitable, yet money is one of its currencies. The muse doesn't value money. Still, money can help the muse indirectly.

In a sidelong way, these thoughts came to me as I was reading *The Gift of Tongues: Twenty-Five Years of Poetry From Copper Canyon Press*, edited by Sam Hamill. Issued in 1996 to mark the press's first quarter-century of poetry publishing, this anthology of poems by Copper Canyon authors emphasizes a certain largeness of spirit. And yet the introduction, written by Hamill, the press's founding editor, also makes a clear case for humility as an essential guide to life, publishing, and writing. Hamill's saga of notably limited means as a worthy path to fulfillment is striking for a banner lack of grandiosity. Over time he has contrived, or so it would seem, to make more and more of scant resources, with some help from his funders, his staff, and his friends. Or, as Hamill put it:

> For the first fifteen or more years of the press, I would not only be an unpaid editor, but as co-publisher with Tree Swenson, would have to find means for paying paper, printing, binding, and mailing bills, as well as other general overhead. Neither of us would derive a livable wage from the press for nearly two decades, and I still do not. I would come to see my work as part of a gift to poetry.

On a suitably humble note, it might be clarifying to think some more about poetry, money, and idealism—about the cost and value of poetry.

⚔

"THE MERE MENTION OF POETRY brings on deficits," says Michael Wiegers, managing editor of Copper Canyon, with an unrepentant snicker. He elaborates, "Because print runs for poetry books are always low, the per book cost is always high." Though Wiegers is idealistic enough to have thrown in his professional lot with poetry, he is also pragmatic enough to think often about money without guilt. "Poetry is slow," he cautions cheerfully. "Poetry forces you to slow down how you breathe, how you think, and therefore how you sell poetry. A poetry best-seller is any book that sells four or five copies in any given store."

Perhaps poetry of late has not been slow enough, Wiegers suggests, with an iconoclast's nonprofit glee. Increasingly an object of promotional zeal since the invention of National Poetry Month in 1995, poetry and its "editing, its marketing, everything—has speeded up, not necessarily for the better," he warns. National Poetry Month, launched under the aegis of the Academy of American Poets, helps to turn a spotlight on poetry each year for the month of April, inspiring readings, performances, lectures, and countless other events across the country, with newspaper, radio, TV, electronic, and magazine coverage to follow. During a recent April, for instance, New Yorkers could pick up free copies of *The Waste Land* at the post office on tax day, thanks to the wry-minded organizational hustle of the Academy, which devised the giveaway. Or, in April of 1998, one could go to hear Laurie Anderson, Jimmy Breslin, and other famous people read their favorite poems at New York City's Town Hall. Even Jay Leno has occasionally caved in and made room for poetry on his talk show. And the entrepreneurial vision of the poets and their publicists can lead to material gains for poetry. In 1997, for example, the Barnes & Noble bookstore chain reported a 30 percent rise in sales of poetry titles for the year, due in part to intensified public activities related to poets and poetry. Directly or less so, National Poetry Month has probably provided Barnes & Noble with some assistance.

However, insists Wiegers, the success of salesmanship in its various guises does have annoying and fulsome drawbacks. "What's being sold now in poetry," he points out, "is the sound bite. Crappy books are getting huge media attention. What's being sold is not the poetry but the writers' stories," along with their would-be celebrity. "Poetry has become fashionable," he regrets, "and not enough work is getting attention for its literary merit. People aren't sitting down to read the words. The commitment is to merchandising, not to poetry," he concludes glumly, as many an idealist would.

In the midst of all this, Wiegers views "Copper Canyon's role in poetry publishing as activist. We're not in it for the merchandising. We're in it from a commitment to poetry, which thumbs its nose at the commodification of art."

Still, many purists and most editors of poetry, even including Wiegers, must concern themselves with conundrums besides purity and editing. One such conundrum is sources of income.

To offset past, current, and expected future losses in support from foundations and corporations that are retreating from funding literature generously, Copper Canyon, like other nonprofit literary organizations responding to that philanthropic trend, has turned to private donors for new or beefed-up contributions to the press's $500,000 annual budget. Says Wiegers, "We operate on such a small scale that it would only take one angel" to give Copper Canyon the financial independence it needs. "If Bill Gates were to set us up with a two million dollar endowment, then Copper Canyon could publish in perpetuity," he dreams. "But we don't have any confidence that it will happen. New money doesn't bring with it the culture of philanthropy," Wiegers sighs, not even when the American economy seems impeccably resurgent. "We're not a saving nation," he laments. "If we don't have the foresight to save for our bank accounts, we may not have the foresight to save for our cultural bank accounts."

Since 1996 the press has begun to focus on fund-raising from plural individuals, and in two years that effort has paid off: total donor contributions to Copper Canyon in that time have come to equal one of the grants the press once depended on but eventually lost, through no fault of its own. In addition, public events have raised money for the press, ranging from a sold-out literary bus tour of Seattle hosted by local writers to a raffle of archival literary first editions and manuscripts at $25 per ticket. (Cautions editor Wiegers: "One of my worries is that this kind of thing gets us away from publishing books.")

Benefits alone have accounted for meeting 15 percent of the press's recent fund-raising goals. In 1996 Copper Canyon began staging a series of benefits in various American cities, using the company's twenty-fifth anniversary celebration as a theme to attract new audiences and to confirm old loyalties. A weeklong roster of events in Seattle earned the press more than $7,000, after expenses of $1,000 had been covered. A similar week in New York during the fall of 1996 cost $4,000 to produce—and only broke even. "People in Seattle know us in a sense that New York doesn't," noted Wiegers, since Copper Canyon is based in nearby Port Townsend, Washington, "and there's also less competition for events in Seattle. Our expectations for New York were a little lower. There's a perception that there's more money in New York, but it's also more expensive. Mainly, our New York week was meant for building a new constituency and for raising our profile. I'd like to return to New York to stage more events. It would be nice to have the recognition in New York that we have now in Seattle."

Recognition, suggests Joe Parisi, the editor of *Poetry* magazine, depends in large part on the power of publicity. "In this economy and in this culture, publicity *equals* money," he says lugubriously. And the key for poets to "earning" publicity (and therefore money) is to give readings from their published work. Alan Thomas, senior editor at the University of Chicago Press, agrees with Parisi. "Readings are *the* way to sell books," he concurs. "People want to hear the poetry before they buy the book—the book may become a memento of the event."

Publicity is primarily the poet's job, not the publisher's, comments Randy Petilos, managing editor of the Phoenix Poets Series published by the University of Chicago Press. "The Press can do only so much for a book—advertise, send out notices, mention the book conversationally." What the Press cannot do is fund poets' author tours, no matter how critical these are to selling books. Nor can most university and small presses. Poets who are members of the academic network will fare best in arranging remunerative gigs for themselves at far-flung colleges and allied venues. Poets who do not teach will find themselves working at a disadvantage, and should—advises Petilos—consider hiring a publicist to begin work on marketing their book six months before it is published.

Fees for readings vary. Not everyone can command $30,000 for a single reading engagement. This is Maya Angelou's standard fee, according to *Forbes* magazine, which in May of 1996 reported her annual income as $4.3 million. But Petilos believes the fees themselves are not so consequential either to a poet or to a publisher. Instead he pays attention to the correlation between readings and book sales. That connection is important.

FOUR MILLION DOLLARS A YEAR? Whatever would a poet need so much money for?

"There's a myth," offers poet Robert Polito, "that there's absolutely no money in poetry—that it's a pure form, detached from money. But once poets became sought after by universities as teachers, money began to matter in a big way. I think universities are very aware of the monetary value of their poets and writers. People aren't making money on the poetry per se, but some are making a lot of money because they're poets. This is a system of indirect reward. It's all part of celebrity culture."

Polito is director of the creative writing program at the New School for Social Research in New York. The program hires no full-time faculty. But "every major university has between one and three tenured poets, many of whom earn at least $80,000 a year—which means a couple hundred total in the United States. *Shouldn't* poetry and poets be compensated and valued?" he asks.

Mark Wunderlich wouldn't disagree with Polito that poets deserve their due in all respects. A poet himself, Wunderlich has contrived an interesting way to help other poets profit while he earns an income from this. He offers poets clerical assistance in selecting and formatting their manuscripts and also provides editorial guidance in submitting the manuscripts for publication to magazines and book publishers. Wunderlich chooses which poems to submit and decides where to submit them; he'll also lick the stamps.

"I see what I do as being a coach," he says. "Most people turn to me because they hate or fear sending out their work. To have an intermediary doing it for them makes the process seem a lot less intimidating."

Wunderlich's rates range from $12 an hour for "basic paperwork" to $20 for "higher-level consulting," such as making editorial comments about a manuscript. "My work is incredibly portable with a computer and modem and fax. I've traveled a lot in the last several years, bringing work with me wherever I am."

Thanks to his efforts, some of Wunderlich's clients have seen their poems accepted by the *Virginia Quarterly Review* and the *New England Review,* among others. On average, four hours of work on his part were required for any one acceptance. Unlike agents, Wunderlich does not charge a percentage fee for any sale of poetry that he arranges. "I get paid whether the poems get published or not."

He began his business in 1992. In 1996, he earned $5,000 from it. Wunderlich agrees that there is an irony to be found in making money from poetry when poetry itself rarely makes any. "But I have to say that I've only ever worked for people who could afford to pay me, just as they'd pay anyone to perform a service for them. People are willing to pay not to worry about this thing."

Any intangible benefits? "My work as a consultant has made me approach dealing with my own poetry in a much more business-like way."

⚒

"THE PROBLEM WITH POETRY," groans an editor who works with poets at a leading New York trade house, "is it's outside of the capitalist economy. One of the worst symptoms of this is that all our poets send out a zillion complimentary copies of their books to other poets. I feel like saying to them, 'Why don't you *buy* the fucking things?' Poetry is booming, but it isn't really translating into sales of books. Sales are definitely doing better, but . . . it's really frustrating to think that poetry will always need this life support.

"A good book," the editor points out, "will give you thirty hours of pleasure for $22. A movie gives you two hours of pleasure for $8. The problem is that reading isn't a social activity. That's what poetry readings are designed to redress."

However, Octavio Paz has written, "Poetry is the antidote to technology and the market." He continues,

In a world ruled by the logic of the marketplace, or in Communist countries by state planning, poetry is an activity that brings no return whatsoever. Its products

are scarcely saleable and very nearly useless.... Yet
against all odds, poetry circulates and is read.

Is poetry booming? As a result of promotional activity held at
bookstores around the country during the opening season of
National Poetry Month in April of 1996, many booksellers noticed
leaps in sales of poetry books. At Bibelot in Baltimore, sales rose 35
percent in April. During the twelve months following, that level of
sales continued more or less unimpaired. At Shaman Drum in
Ann Arbor, Michigan, sales for the month rose 30 to 40 percent.
Clemson Newsstand in Clemson, South Carolina, saw sales
double. Borders Books and Music promoted selected poetry titles,
and sales of these titles rose as much as 150 percent. Barnes &
Noble recorded sales increases for poetry of 100 percent, tops, for
the month of April. And at City Lights bookstore in San Francisco,
hardcover poetry sales soared 68 percent in 1996. Poetry sales in
April of 1997 also thrived, with increases cited at Prairie Lights
Books in Iowa City (20 percent), A Clean Well-Lighted Place for
Books in Larkspur, California (35 percent), and Davis-Kidd
Booksellers in Nashville (40 percent), among others.

Individual titles, as always, find their own destinies. *The Spirit
Level*, Seamus Heaney's 1996 collection of poetry (Farrar, Straus and
Giroux, $18), had sold 20,000 copies by the end of that year, due
partly to his 1995 Nobel prize. Hayden Carruth's *Scrambled Eggs
& Whiskey: Poems 1991–1995* (Copper Canyon Press, $25 cloth, $14
paper) had sold 13,000 copies as of early 1997. Carruth's book, which
received the National Book Award for poetry in 1996, increased
Copper Canyon's sales by 25 percent in the year of the award.

But the standard sales expectation for hardcover poetry published
by Farrar, Straus and Giroux is a 5,000 first printing sold out over

the course of a year. For the University of Chicago Press's Phoenix Poets Series, which is published entirely in paperback, 1,400 copies sold over three or four years is usual. At Northwestern University Press, a 200 cloth and 1,500 paper run are typical, "and if it sells over 1,000 copies, we do better than break even," says NUP director Nick Weir-Williams. Assuming that a poet gives readings twice each month over the span of a year, this will lead to sales of from twenty to fifty copies a month, Weir-Williams says. "Our poetry sales have mostly outdone our fiction, and have certainly outdone our essay collections. I think poetry is cost-effective. The internal costs of publishing it are very small."

STILL, IT IS RARE FOR ANY POET to redeem a publisher financially. One of the few to have done so is the late Jane Kenyon. Kenyon's *Otherwise: New and Selected Poems* ($23.95 cloth, $16 paper) was published in hardcover by the Graywolf Press in April of 1996 and has sold more than 22,000 copies in hardcover during the two years since. The paperback edition, published in September of 1997, sold 13,000 in its first eighteen months. Graywolf, where I have been a contributing editor since 1995, had also published several of Kenyon's previous books. Total sales of those combined with *Otherwise* came to 68,700 copies by April of 1998.

"*Otherwise* contributed more financially to Graywolf than any other book in 1996," says Fiona McCrae, Graywolf's director. "If you take the long view and commit to a poet, publishing them over a series of years, then it's entirely consistent that you get an economic reward. Taking the long view can be very sound economic reasoning, and not just literary. Maybe that's what the nonprofit status can allow a press to do more easily. When you're asked to turn a profit in a short time, you haven't got time to wait."

One of the book's subjects—depression—may also be responsible for the popularity of *Otherwise*. Tom Bevan, director of marketing and promotion at the Academy of American Poets, keeps a copy near his bed. "I read a few poems before I go to sleep," he says. "They let you know that the worst things you feel are felt by others, yet the poems also let you feel better about where you are. I think people *like* depressing poems. I do. If you can get a perspective on depression, then you can rise above it."

Another boon of *Otherwise* is the poetry's ease of access to readers. "She's such an approachable writer," observes Lisa Bullard, Graywolf's marketing director. "Kenyon somehow strikes a common chord, and people respond to it. And then there's also the morbid fact that an artist's work tends to do well after they've died. Her death did have an impact. There was a lot of press coverage, and people really wanted the book because it was the last Jane Kenyon book they could have. They were moved by her death."

Or, as Graywolf sales and rights director Janna Rademacher puts it, "She's the only poet we have who transcends the poetry audience and reaches non-poetry readers. A lot of *Otherwise*'s success happened because she passed away. So, success is tragic."

McCrae points to the importance of Bill Moyers's Emmy award-winning TV program, *A Life Together*, about Kenyon and her husband, the poet Donald Hall, in introducing her to a broad audience not only as a writer but also as a person. Hall himself did much to spread word of the poet and her book at various readings he gave from *Otherwise* and in interviews, some of them broadcast on radio. (He continued to bring her to mind when reading in 1998 from his own new book of poetry, *Without*, which concerns

Kenyon, her death, and his survival.) A series of memorials also evoked Kenyon in a special light. Meanwhile, some of her poems were appearing in *The New Yorker.* "It's a book that didn't need reviews to sell," notes Bullard. Yet the reviews were acclamatory in the *Washington Post, The New Yorker,* and finally in the *New York Times Book Review.* Pulitzer prize–winning composer William Bolcom even created a song cycle based on nine of Kenyon's poems. The piece, "Briefly It Enters," debuted in Ann Arbor and later traveled to San Francisco, New Hampshire, Wisconsin, and New York City.

Perhaps most remarkable of all, the paperback sales of Kenyon's early Graywolf books "have still been good even with *Otherwise* in print," Bullard says. "The previous books have done phenomenally, though most of those poems are included in *Otherwise.* People seem to want every book she has ever published."

⚰

WHEN YOU REALLY WANT POETRY, covet it, pine for it, to what lengths will you go to get it? The value of poetry to you can be inferred from the number of library books you check out and renew, from the number of readings you attend, from the number of books you buy or poetry classes you enroll in. But the value of poetry can also be imagined by studying the perverse career of a plagiarist who steals poems.

Poet Neil Bowers's book, *Words for the Taking: The Hunt for a Plagiarist* (W. W. Norton, 1997), recounts his experience of being plagiarized over a long period by one man, then of pursuing the plagiarist, trying to see some little justice done, and more or less failing. *Words for the Taking* is a beguiling read, not only because of the story's surprises, suspense, and idiosyncrasies, but also for the accumulation of meaning that accrues gradually to plagiarism as a metaphor for worth of property.

Plagiarism suggests a criminal activity and the plagiarist's possible insanity. Presumably a plagiarist sets high store in whatever he plagiarizes—that is why he claims ownership of it. Even so, why would anyone steal poetry, which to a thief conveys very little material advantage? Of what value is poetry to him, and why does he want to steal it?

"People have told me I should be flattered by the thefts," Bowers says ruefully. "But I always feel sullied. Some of my friends even tell me, 'Well, the plagiarist *hasn't* stolen your property. You still have it!' But I do have to reclaim the poems that were stolen and published under his name. I have to say insistently and defiantly that yes, they are my poems."

Bowers hasn't written any poetry about the plagiarist, although "quite a few of my friends and students have. Brendan Galvin did." Instead, in Words for the Taking he focused on telling the tale of the plagiarist in conversational prose, putting his own poetry aside for quite a while. "I may have been trying to protect my poetry from the plagiarist by not writing any," he speculates. But in a roundabout way, even his poetic losses have offered some rewards to Bowers the poet.

He struggled in writing Words for the Taking with the challenge of constructing a narrative—an especially difficult task for a lyric poet. Yet in the end, the confidence and skill he gained in storytelling has helped his poetry, leading Bowers to complete the centerpiece of his next collection, a long autobiographical narrative poem about racism and his Southern boyhood. "The story I tell in the poem is really told at my own expense," he says. "I'm very much exposed." This was a breakthrough, he believes.

So, however oddly, Bowers has been able to extract some value from his experience of poetry robbery. The mishap leaves him reconsidering the usual value of poetry. "The poet is a person," Bowers offers, "who takes a certain responsibility on himself to say those things that other people are reluctant or unable to say. The poet is someone who makes himself vulnerable by saying, 'I have felt this way.' Poetry is a way of communicating with other people — of getting over those walls we have between us. All poetry begins with the poet trying to understand himself."

In 1934, Marianne Moore commented on the value of poetry and the propriety of profit in a letter to T. S. Eliot.

> I am sure it is true there is not money in poetry for anybody and to say that I dislike the thought of being a loss to a publisher is far more than a mere understatement. I have known for a long time that I ought not to plan to live on money derived from authorship. The writing in itself pays one or something is wrong with it.

# Margaret Amanuensis

"NOTHING HAS EVER BEEN MORE DELIGHTFUL than the California rainy season spent in this rather exotic fashion," wrote Margaret Anderson during her early life as an editor. The year was 1916. "In the mornings I rode my horse through the dripping forests to the inn at the heart of Muir Woods, filled my knapsack with provisions, and came back to find Jane making biscuits for lunch. Afterward we covered the table with *Little Review* work. I had never found any pleasure in answering the letters that came in, usually accompanied by bad manuscripts. I hid them away like a squirrel in inaccessible places.

"But Jane adored writing to people. Her first idea in joining the *Little Review* was to be its amanuensis. She spent her time answering letters with exaggerated interest (real) and in planning new typographies which we could never afford. I planned forthcoming issues, especially those filled with articles I meant to extract from Jane. After tea we walked under the misty eucalyptus trees, chiefly for the comfort of returning to the fire-lit room. Then we dressed elaborately in pajamas, discussed sensuous plans for dinner, and prepared it in a kitchen lighted only by a kerosene lamp. . . ."

Though little mentioned now, Anderson was legendary among editors and writers for the power of her whims. She began publishing the *Little Review*, a monthly literary magazine, in 1914 and edited it until 1929, first in Chicago, then in California, next in New York, and finally abroad.

Her friend Janet Flanner said of her, "Lawless by nature, she always practiced a variety of polite anarchy as her basis of conduct." When Anderson's cash-poor but esteemed magazine floundered periodically, for example, she thought nothing of riding to the top of the largest skyscraper in sight and then working her way down from office to office, raising funds as she went. When she could no longer afford to keep her Chicago apartment, she moved north to the shores of Lake Michigan and lived for a time in a tent.

In the course of things, she serialized *Ulysses* for three years running in the pages of her magazine, until she was tried and fined $100 for obscenity. Also published in the *Little Review* under her tenure were Djuna Barnes, Jean Cocteau, Richard Aldington, Ezra Pound, Tristan Tzara, T. S. Eliot, and Louis Aragon.

Meanwhile, Anderson contrived to remain "always exquisite . . . her fluffy hair blows marvelously," as a male admirer put it. In search of full-time euphoria and fluffiness, the rebellious Indiana native finally flung herself and her lover, the singer Georgette Leblanc, to France in 1923, when she was twenty-seven. There she "spent twenty years in five of the more celestial French chateaux. . . . France allowed us to live our secret formulas." Like a kind of literary flapper, she "always wore the right white glove and removed the left white glove so that she could hold her lighted cigarette in her favorite hand which was her left," Flanner noticed. "Then through absent-mindedness she usually lost the lefthand glove."

Anderson claimed to her friends that she could be nothing more than an editor. Yet anyone who reads her three-volume autobiography will recognize her as an impresario whose major work may have been herself. She was also her own best possible amanuensis, a diva who chose to write her life expansively and loudly. Like most divas, Anderson tinkered with the facts, improving on them. As a romantic, she had to do that; it was obligatory. She gave mouth to whatever she felt like, and the result was a festooning myth.

In the early days of her editorship, Anderson was by her own account "so breathless" that "the gesture I made most often (unconscious on my part) was to place my left hand, fingers outspread, against my heart. I must have felt that it had stopped beating and needed my protection. When I was made conscious of the gesture I stopped making it."

In fact, her heart kept beating because "I was born to be an editor. I always edit everything," she insisted. "I edit my room at least once a week."

To follow the story in her own words is to billow in a wake of flummery and fanaticism, quickened by an old-fashioned quest for art without which there was little else worth having. Anderson must have been more shrewd than she now sounds to have kept the *Little Review* in business for a decade and a half. If you can bear her prose's oracular chariot-swings, then the retro ride is exhilarating, unbeholden to paper clips, spreadsheets, or floppy disks.

"We didn't pass through thought to arrive at opinion," she declared in volume two of her autobiography, "we leapt to resplendent conclusions." She meant herself and her erstwhile coeditor, Anderson's flame, memorably named Jane Heap. "We

were the people who knew things without learning them; we were
the producers, rather than the product, of experience."

Margaret's deviant effervescent breathlessness, though, did
need to find recurrent resting places. She found them in the
people whom she talked about or at.

Reported M. with Jane from Paris, "Hemingway is a rabbit—
white and pink face, soft brown eyes that look at you without
blinking. As for his love for boxing and bull-fighting—all that is
thrashing up the ground with his hind legs." Anderson admired
the way he had trained his small child "in coordination by teach-
ing it to thrust out its hand and catch passing flies." She rather
liked Hemingway also, at least until he began to chase her.

She was willing to give advice to confused young artists
distracted by follies much like hers. Visited by one of them, an
American girl who seemed the worse for something, Anderson
was asked, "What shall I do to become a good writer?"

Anderson replied: "First disabuse yourself of the national idea
that genius is a capacity for hard work. . . . The meaning of genius
is that it doesn't have to work to attain what people without it
must labor for—and not attain."

The girl wailed, "Yes, but what shall I do?"

Anderson: "Use a little lip rouge, to begin with. Beauty may
bring you experiences to write about."

She met and published everyone from Francis Picabia to
Edgar Lee Masters.

"Edgar Lee Masters was the funny man of the [Chicago]
literati. His eyes twinkled (it's the only verb) and he indulged with
obvious pleasure in the lowest slap-stick humor," she revealed.
"Francis Picabia had become French editor of the *Little Review*

in 1922 but we never had anything from him except a Picabia number," she whined.

Volume one of her autobiography is relatively rational and hard-headed, telling mainly of Anderson's ups and downs with her magazine. "We hired the cheapest printer in New York," she wrote, "Mr. Popovitch, whose mother had been poet laureate of Serbia. He had two daughters. They all took a personal interest in the magazine. We went to their shop in [sic] East Twenty-third Street and helped with the setting-up, to gain time—and lost much time helping the daughters to read Wyndham Lewis."

Volume two, which takes up her French exile and love affair with Leblanc, mocks the French aristocratic parsimony on show at the chilly castles where she and her girlfriend usually stayed. Anderson liked writing in order to quarrel with someone or something—said frozen aristocrats, or the insulted Hoosiers of her birthplace.

But the largely formless joy of her unmoored life abroad, influenced by her studies with the mystic Gurdjieff, makes for some fairly unshaped arabesques. "My unaccountable inner happiness has always been almost too much for me," she confessed. "I never had time enough to live it out, to live it down.... Naturally I had hardships, but I thought they were illusions.... I have never been too hungry or too tired, too ill or too cold, too ugly or too wrong, too crowded or too alone."

By volume three, the shapelessness has given way to something else—a breathlessness that is running out of breath. "My life is a mystery, even to myself," Anderson solemnly informed that self.

Still, as she had promised in her youth, "I won't be cornered and I won't stay suppressed."

# Lorrie "Metaphor" Moore

IN THE GORGEOUS WILDERNESS of Lorrie Moore's fiction, you will find posted sentries: similes and metaphors. There are more of them in this fiction than in many poems, and the fact intrigues me. The gush of metaphorical figures contributes to her power of monologue and display. The metaphors and similes can also distract a reader. They suggest a map of choices made by the author, diversions for us in the course of reading. Yet "diversion" is too trivial and lackluster a word to describe the impact of the figures. No—if to read her is like taking a try at orienteering in an unfamiliar forest, then Moore's similes and metaphors are like quick changes of light in a driving, witful wind.

Oddly, her writing sometimes tempts me to do without simile and metaphor in my own. Reading her, I feel chagrined by my former use of them. My past efforts at selection now feel awkward, self-conscious, lacking in freedom. Moore has something in common with John Ashbery in her conniptious, dizzying, dancelike panoply of things evoked and rhythms assayed. One can't mimic this; you have to come up short. Her rhythms are usually bound to the free fall of a singular self (whether this is a first-person narrator or not). And, as with Ashbery, they are concerned with comic permutations of that self.

Early in her novel *Who Will Run the Frog Hospital?* (Knopf, 1994), Moore's willfully unruly heroine confides to us:

> When I was a child, I tried hard for a time to split my voice. I wanted to make chords, to splinter my throat into harmonies—floreted as a field, which is how I saw it. It seemed like something one should be able to do. With concentration and a muscular push of air, I felt, I might be able to people myself, unleash the crowd in my voice box, give birth, set free all the moods and nuances, all the lovely and mystical inhabitants of my mind's speech.... There must have been pain in me. I wanted to howl and fly and break apart.

The effect of splitting the harmonies of a voice is felt often in Moore's work as a bombardment of sensibility, an unleashing of various "moods and nuances." And the sensibility is expressed partly in her array of figurative language, which should be exemplary for poets. The densely loopy wash of words carries the pain of anomie, but tenderly enough that the pain is subtle and usually unnamed. I'm reluctant, from respect for the writing, to characterize or corner the pain.

My delight with Moore's libertine love of metaphor partly consoles me in my dismay at metaphor's momentary malaise in contemporary American poetry. Of course, metaphor hasn't vanished entirely; that wouldn't be permitted. Yet metaphor has too frequently become a duly expected part of the poem—obedient, unsurprising, rotely constituent. In Moore's paragraphs and pages, however, metaphor is wild, big, and rampant. She has things to teach poets that we haven't already taught ourselves.

Glimpse a few of Moore's metaphors and similes, and marvel at their lucid, hybrid madness:

Planted in large, gorgeous ovals are tulips so big that they look as if they'd steal your jewelry.

"Do you think the Venus de Milo looks like Nicolas Cage?"

I knew the Bible like my own closet (Leviticus 14:10! Green knit crochet vest!).

The year before, every third Sunday, while my parents attended the service, I had helped baby-sit in the Baptist church nursery—a large pink room with cribs at one end; at the other hung an enormous gold-framed painting of Jesus, whose upward gaze and caramel-colored locks gave him the look of a dewy Kenny Loggins.

In the morning she warmed her arms over the blue zinnias of the gas jets.

*I hope you are not wearing those new, puffy evening dresses I see in magazines. They make everyone look like sticky buns.*

The darkness was thick and certain, not a shaded,
waltzing dark but a paralyzing coffin jet.

Love without intimacy, she knew, was an unsung tune.

The first four quotations come from *Who Will Run the Frog
Hospital?* and the rest from Moore's short story "The Jewish Hunter."

"The Jewish Hunter," collected in *Like Life* (Knopf, 1990), is
about a New York City poet named Odette who is sent to be an artist-
in-residence in a midwestern town where "people took things
literally" and where there were "gyms but no irony or coffee shops."
Odette, needless to say, is herself no literalist; Moore's story about her
glints with metaphorically intensified language. Still, despite
Odette's skepticism about literalism and her longstanding loyalty to
poetry, she comes to experience a temporary change of heart.
Meeting and falling in love with a mostly wholesome local lawyer
named Pinky Eliot during her out-of-town stint, she settles into a
literary decline and even comes to doubt her own New Yorker–
desperado turn of mind—which seems akin to Moore's own—but
recovers and returns east, in the end. One symptom of her decline:
she abandons writing her usual sort of poetry and instead begins
penning limericks about hookers, reciting them at public libraries for
the dubious benefit of elderly women wielding "botched knitting."
Moore is satirizing poetic pretension, as well as the fate of people in
small midwestern towns who know little if anything about it. Her
satire calls forth a stream of figurative language to make the point
(and to feed poetry with some potent, antic vitamins).

The cascade of metaphors and similes in the story is virtuosic,
yet not offered just for virtuosity's sake. Instead, the language
seems to serve as a measure of possibility, suggesting what a poet

might do if she were truly canny and resourceful. And Moore's challenging metaphors pose questions: what is Odette's poetry meant for, really? Is it equipped to represent real life? Is the poetry even interested in this? Shouldn't it be? The sensory litheness of the metaphorical language evokes the extremes of experience that are likely for us—extremes contradictory, bombarding, and often beyond our rational understanding.

As if wooed by a more persuasive reality than poetry has so far provided her with, Odette comes close to giving poetry up for the ingenuous charms of a man who finds her writing "a little too literaturey for me." In the slippery speed-lurches of the story, Moore maybe wants to catch out a poet who's been quite busy with writing her life glibly. Rather too glibly, could it be? Or is Odette's oily New York habit of monomaniacal perpetual articulation a wholly necessary tic?

Pinky, the literalist and nice guy, can't fathom the tic. And under his influence, the frantic narcissism of Odette's ceaseless song-spiel at times lights (with metaphor's help) on something like transcendent truth:

He closed his eyes and kissed her, long and slow, and she left her sunglasses on so she could keep her eyes open and watch, see how his lashes closed on one another like petals, how his scar zoomed quiet and white about his cheek and chin, how his lips pushed sleepily against her own to find a nest in hers and to stay there, moving, as if in words, but then not in words at all, his hands going round her in a soft rustle, up the back of her sweater to her bare waist and spine, and spreading there, blooming large and holding her just briefly until he pulled away, gathered himself back to himself, and quietly shifted the car into drive.

The metaphorical description is almost more important than the loving here, though not quite. Moore tells us how Odette expects and accepts love: first in words, and then as if in words, until it's all too clear that words won't suffice.

Which isn't to suggest that we ought to forget about words, or about metaphor. My contrary, puritanical urge to shuck metaphor sometimes after reading Moore may have been perversely nudged by her conviction, implied above, that words may not be enough to evoke or account for life—nothing is—and therefore, paradoxically, one should make the most of words, however tumultuous the writing then becomes. Unlike some poets, Moore isn't a believer in the propriety of metaphor, only in the vitality of metaphor. She mixes her metaphors without regrets.

At another illustrative moment in "The Jewish Hunter," Odette and Pinky visit a cave on a date.

> "Please do not touch the formations," the cave tour guide kept shouting over everyone's head. Along the damp path through the cave there were lights, which allowed you to see walls marbled a golden rose, like a port cheddar; nippled projections, blind galleries, arteries all through the place, chalky and damp; stalagmites and stalactites in walrusy verticals, bursting up from the floor in yearning or hanging wicklessly in drips from the ceiling, making their way, through time, to the floor. The whole cave was in a weep, everything wet and slippery; still ocher pools of water bordered the walk, which spiraled gradually down. "Nature's Guggenheim," said Odette.

The procession of mixed metaphors would seem to establish a new rule to entice us: finicky license.

Also unlike some poets, Moore doesn't abide by the common hierarchy giving preferred status to metaphor and a slightly inferior position to simile. Her way is to layer them intermittently like stings of perception that are too bright.

She disrupts and reinvents poetic prospects as though she had no choice.

⚓

But Moore's loyalty to metaphor is more than a source of delight. Her riotous prose offers American poetry a lesson or two. At a time when heightened figurative language has fallen out of fashion among poets, many of whom seem to prefer the exclusive, egocentric onrush of post-confessionalism, Moore offers us metaphor renewed and Dionysian in the safe haven of her paragraphs.

What kind of safety can a paragraph provide? The reprieve of prose for anyone who dreads meeting a poem. Readers who would normally fear verse (and poets who avoid figuration) stumble unexpectedly in her prose upon Moore's poetry. Disarmed, charmed, and perhaps persuaded that rich language isn't something to snub or to scoff at, an explorer of her fiction finds verbal feints, flights, and ornate traceries to be as real as any true-life plot. Also, the plot is rightly receptive to the feints. With abandon Moore restores to metaphor an earthly significance.

Nowhere is this clearer than in her short story "People Like That Are the Only People Here," published in *The New Yorker* in 1996 and included in Moore's most recent collection of short fiction, *Birds of America* (Knopf, 1998). "People Like That Are the Only People Here" approaches heady new extremes, new even for Moore, in the story's clambering journey with language, and suggests with an unfamiliar ferocity the splurges acceptable to metaphor. Unlike many poets now, Moore surprisingly places metaphor at the center of her action, as if it mattered as much as any narrator.

Metaphors test and prove the mettle of the distressed main character in the story, a mother whose very young child has been diagnosed with a malignant kidney tumor. The story begins with her discovery of his symptom and follows the family through his diagnosis, surgery, and early stages of recovery. Throughout, metaphors are primarily responsible for expressing—and sometimes for furiously protesting—emotional reality. As before, let's consider a small catalogue of Moore's figures:

The Mother knows her own face is a big white dumpling of worry.

The Mother finds a blood clot in the Baby's diaper. What is the story? Who put this here? It is big and bright, with a broken, khaki-colored vein in it. Over the weekend, the Baby had looked listless and spacey, clayey and grim. But today he looks fine—so what is this thing, startling against the white diaper, like a tiny mouse heart packed in snow?

He has grown so much in the last year he hardly fits in her lap anymore; his limbs dangle off like a Pietà.

"If you go," she keens low into his soapy neck, into the ranunculus coil of his ear, "we are going with you."

Swirls of bile and blood, mustard and maroon in a pail, the colors of an African flag or some exuberant salad bar....

Think of leukemia, a tumor diabolically taking liquid form, the better to swim about incognito in the blood. George Lucas, direct that!

"A little light chemo. Don't you like that one?" says the Mother. "*Eine kleine* dactinomycin. I'd like to see Mozart write that one up for a big wad o' cash."

But strangely optimistic codas are tacked on: endings as stiff and loopy as carpenter's lace, crisp and empty as lettuce, reticulate as a net—ah, words.

The mouth itself, working at the speed of light, at the eye's instructions, is necessarily struck still; so fast, so much to report, it hangs open and dumb as a gutted bell. All that unsayable life! That's where the narrator comes in. The narrator comes with her kisses and mimicry and tidying up. The narrator comes and makes a slow, fake song of the mouth's eager devastation.

Because she can't explain what's happening to her family or bear to think of what may happen next, the mother's metaphors indirectly do the thinking and explaining for her, with breathtaking accuracy and confidence. The poignance of their moral and literary victory comes from our understanding of their tender source in the mother's rage, her confusion, her terror, and her foreseeable losses. The shock of the metaphors as they enjoy an impact on us resembles the successive shocks felt by the mother as her son sickens. The metaphors also fight back in favor of life when life is threatened. Moore's aggressively sardonic juxtapositions in her metaphorical comparisons (blood with mustard, African nationalism with American lunches, and Mozart with therapeutic poison) pound on us with good reason: their bitter absurdity echoes the injustice of the toddler's (and mother's) trauma. Yet at the same time, metaphor liberates the mother humanely from the monstrous responsibility of having simply to "tell." No confession is possible for her or anyone else, because life has interrupted their stories with the swarm of its own. In panic and disgust, the narrator revokes her role, and hands it over to metaphor.

Even more than Moore's others, the story outdoes poets at their linguistic game. And it would be worthwhile for poets to heed her example. If it seems odd for us to look to a fiction writer for guidance, especially in matters of verbal mastery, then perhaps certain generational inadequacies lead us to her.

The generational inadequacies on my mind are associated with contemporary poetic confessionalism, that too-much-admired offspring of an heroic recent past. Since its vigorous beginnings with Robert Lowell, W. D. Snodgrass, Anne Sexton, John Berryman, and others, the movement has rippled through the ranks of countless students and writers of mixed abilities and desires. What they've had in common is the urge to divulge something painful, personal, and factual in writing; after telling all, they're freed, ostensibly—or at least appeased spiritually. Their pain has been shed because it's been shared. That seems to be a governing purpose of the poetry.

And yet language itself doesn't necessarily benefit from confession, whether because the subject of the poem compels the writer's main attention, or from another cause. Unless the linguistic stakes are somehow raised by exceptional writers, confessionalism can and does become a sentimental and belabored business. Its language often seems too busy with carrying the burden of confession—the literal facts of experience, and an outsize, sometimes simplified emotional cargo—to consider or embody richly figurative word choices or the enhanced, complex meanings they signify. Unimaginative, undemanding, confessional poetry may ebb into a sort of prose. Whatever metaphors remain in the standard confessional poem may come across as perfunctory and secondhand, eclipsed by the "larger" factual drama. The recent rise in popularity of prose memoirs, compelled by a similar confessional urge, has done little to dissuade poets—many of them now also memoirists—from interrupting or reconsidering the confessional reflex in their stanzas.

However, Moore rescues metaphor as a primary color for writers. Her metaphors suggest what can't be said nakedly or blatantly; they overcome our insentience in subtler stages. Metaphors also give Moore's fiction an appropriately galvanic emotional texture. They aren't meant to be ornamentally "poetic." Instead, they mimic life at its cruelest and boldest, returning the real to realism.

Would that they—and she—could do the same for poetry and poets.

# The Small Press Muse
# and Its Difficulties

PUBLISHING IS THE BUSINESS OF OPINION.

I wish someone had told me this when I still believed that publishing (especially poetry publishing) was an innately quixotic line of work. Regardless of what I thought, publishing is not quixotic by nature. Nor is it really, as some believe, a kingdom for the worldly and the crass. You can count on little profit and less virtue in publishing. The seed and the crop are: opinion.

Whose opinion, of course, makes all the difference. The range of opinion dictates and distinguishes one-time-only chapbooks, translation series, book imprints, university press publishing programs, and the mind-boggling welter of product management at large trade houses. Despite the range, though, almost any opinion has a funny way of seeming absolute once it has been embodied in a book. At that moment, opinion picks up a seductive weight; it becomes difficult to controvert. An idea has come to something, apparently. A home has been given to a diabolical spark.

Many small presses began as one person's opinion-making organism, and now some of those people are reconsidering their opinions and the organism, or they should be. Widespread cuts in arts funding have brought a quarter century of relative generosity to a pause or a close. The consequences are up to the presses, not the gods.

The muse created for writers by small presses may have mattered more to poets and their readers than to anyone else. Decades ago, that muse was shy, putting in fledgling appearances before a relatively rarefied audience. Since then, many of the poetry books we care most about have emerged from independent publishers with opinions to spare. Not from them exclusively; poetry belongs to no one, and thrives on motley auspices. But all you have to do is scan some book spines to judge the point: the publishing of poetry is largely noncommercial or alternative. A muse that makes little money has no sure place inside a profit-making corporate publishing house.

What can a muse do in response to reduced circumstances? In a speculative mood, I set out in 1996 to collect and reflect on opinions about the state of poetry in small press publishing. Here are a few.

"For poetry, the largest market is the small independent presses," confirms Jim Sitter, from the perspective of his role then as executive director of the Council of Literary Magazines and Presses in New York. "That doesn't mean commercial presses don't publish extremely important work or publish it very well, but you won't see many *new* writers added at those houses. Still," he notes ruefully, "tightening of resources will continue for a number of years regardless. In no way is there any clear path for small presses.

"The donated revenue stream will flatten and narrow down," Sitter anticipates. "Growth will have to continue based on earned income. Smaller, newer presses and magazines will see a ceiling forming as far as subsidy. And book distribution systems have dwindled.

"Traditionally in small press publishing, everything has been built around a single editorial vision seen in opposition to New York corporate publishing. This romantic view of the small presses," Sitter cautions, "has disregarded the economics of publishing and limited all but a handful of small presses from growing to any significant size. Over the last fifteen years, small presses have come to serve poets and poetry in a more sophisticated way. But what they are right now may be as much as they *can* be."

Some small presses are nonprofit; others are for-profit. Some are deliberately fringe or culturally adversarial; others are unmistakably centrist. Some small press publishers are actually opposed to government support of literature, while others have plainly benefited from it and covet more. A small press can be many things. Still, all small presses do have at least one thing in common, according to Rochelle Ratner, executive editor of the *American Book Review*. "In small presses," observes Ratner, "the big difference is that editors are making all the decisions."

Small press publishing has always been surprisingly subject to change. Michael Anania, literary editor of the Swallow Press from 1967 to 1974, remembers small press publishing of the '60s and '70s as "mostly saddle-stitched chapbooks, given 300- or 500-copy press runs. In a sense, these were created to be instant 'rare books.'" The publisher's function was like that of a curator protecting an unusual artifact.

"Then," continues Anania, "with the evolution of the National

Endowment for the Arts literary funding programs, pressures grew from the Endowment and state agencies for small presses to be more effective in production, marketing, and sales." Their standards rose; their books became modeled in some respects on those of university presses and trade publishers, rather than on their own direct progenitors. In the main, according to Anania, this upgrade has been a good thing, yet it includes some subtle pitfalls. He feels especially skeptical about "the professionalization of the nonprofit world," comparing it with the yuppification of some once-marginal urban American neighborhoods, which have since lost their original identity and nerve. In the case of professional nonprofits, he believes, "corporate boards begin to influence what you do, and their interests won't be yours. They won't allow you, as a publisher, to indulge your instincts."

Argues Anania, "The dilemma of American publishing is that we propose again and again to ourselves that literary quality is somehow determined by corporate sponsorship. Just *forget* Random House and the whole lot of them!" he urges. "Why should it be a shock to poets that for them a 'house' like that is not a home?"

Mary Bisbee-Beek, a publicity and marketing consultant who has promoted many small press poetry books from her office in St. Paul, Minnesota, holds a different view. "Past growth in funding for small presses by the Endowment, the Andrew C. Mellon Foundation Fund, and the Lila Wallace–Reader's Digest Fund has been only beneficial," she says. "It hasn't brought a change in spirit to small press publishing, just a change in efficiency. The small presses want to be players. They've woken up." At best, she believes, such grant money showered on small presses should have helped to teach them the benefits of long-term self-sufficiency, educating them in tactics likely to advance this. However, she says, since the more recent decline of literary funding at some major foundations, small presses—especially the more marginal or less established—have been forced to trim their staffs or do work in-house that had previously been freelanced out and paid for by grants. Others have reduced the number of books they can afford to publish each year. "The presses have to work harder to make money now," she observes.

Even so, it's true that some small presses publishing poetry mainly or exclusively—a seemingly hopeless financial proposition— indeed grew during the years of philanthropic plenty.

Two stalwarts among them are Copper Canyon Press of Port Townsend, Washington, and BOA Editions of Brockport, New York. Copper Canyon managing editor Michael Wiegers declares flatly, "Plenty of publishing people think we're nuts to do nothing but poetry, yet that's one of our strongest assets." Over the past decade, Copper Canyon, founded in 1972, has expanded its publishing list from four to ten books a year, due in part to the generosity of outside funders. "Funding has always been unpredictable," Wiegers empha- sizes. "The recent loss of funding certainly doesn't mean we'll close up shop and go away. But we may not be able to do as thorough a job of marketing our books, and then we may need to cut back the number of books we publish. I worry most about the infant presses that may not be able to benefit at all from foundation support. How are we going to nurture new editorial voices, who would in turn nurture new poetic voices?" he asks.

BOA director of marketing and development Thom Ward has watched BOA's list swell from four to eight books a year since 1993, helped by a Wallace grant. He would like to see that number shift eventually to ten. "We try not to outgrow ourselves," he confides.

"It is not easy to sell poetry. The appreciative audience for poetry is growing, but I'm not convinced that the buying audience is." Nonetheless, BOA's annual sales have risen from $72,000 in 1993 to $145,000 in 1995. "Aggressive marketing" by Consortium, BOA's distributor, has played a role in this, Ward says.

Ward cites as one of BOA's disadvantages the ongoing struggle of poetry books in particular to stick it out on bookstore shelves for long enough to find buyers and profit in sales from the positive effects of enthusiastic reviews, author tours, literary prizes, and the old-fashioned push often given to a poetry book by latecoming, informal word-of-mouth recommendations. The books (or some of them) are often returned unsold by the store to the publisher long before then. Independent bookstores, he has found, can be even less patient in granting a book of poetry a long shelf life than are the chain booksellers, due to the usually quite limited shelf space available in the independent stores. "In the old days," Ward reminisces, "an independent bookstore would order eight or ten copies of a poetry book from us, sell five, and keep five" for perpetuity, or virtually. Now the stores tend to order an average of only two or three copies per title.

To compensate for the diminution of big-time national literary funding, Ward advises small presses to seek out greater numbers of individual donors and to explore new potential local funders. Between 1995 and 1997, BOA has tripled its income contributed by donors, partly by attracting fresh recruits. BOA's board is also larger and more active now and helps to raise money for the press. In addition, Ward has seen BOA augment its revenue through subsidiary rights sales — to the tune of $20,000 in a recent fiscal year. To him "slow growth" is a practical goal and a present fact even in the wake of decreased national support for independent nonprofit publishing.

But "literary publishing is an incredibly strange animal," Ward admits. "I'm still learning things after six years of working at it." He genially offers Ward's Hypothesis: "There's maybe five to ten thousand nonprofessional readers of poetry in the country—readers who are not poets themselves. The challenge for publishers is to get more general readers continuously interested in poetry—interested enough to buy it."

When is a poetry reader not a buyer?

Lee Briccetti, executive director of Poets House in New York, a reading room, information center, library, and presenter of poetry events, draws an intriguing distinction between a poet's "audience" and his or her "market." The audience "may be much larger than the market," she proposes, and yet the audience may not contribute directly to poetry's revenue in dollars and cents. Audience members listen, partake of poetry, and help to form poetry's boisterous family—but not to pay for it. Advises Briccetti, "We need to develop a means of advocacy for poetry. The poetry 'audience' has to think of itself as a 'market'—for example, make a point of buying books by small presses. Poets must get beyond the preoccupation with their careers and manuscripts to gain a larger sense of the field and participate in it."

One of those poets who makes a point of participating is Molly Peacock. "I've never edited a magazine or run a small press," she concedes. "I'm a deeply sympathetic observer." She's an observer, though, with quite a specific expertise. President of the Poetry Society of America from 1989 to 1994, as president emerita, Peacock remains an active fund-raiser for the PSA.

She's only too willing to share her fund-raising ideas. "The small presses must find new sources of funding," Peacock offers. "So poets who can, *must* sink money into small press publishing. For a poet to sit back and say, 'Oh, do it all for me!' is reprehensible. I don't. I've bought advertising for my own books, and make no bones about that."

How and where should the presses themselves look for support? "They need to start small. You begin a career in fund-raising with baby steps, just as you begin a career in poetry. I didn't know a thing about fund-raising when I began. But the power of your personality and the power of your friendships are going to work for you. You're attractive because you're *you*—to the people who know you already, and then perhaps to the people who know *them*. The amounts given may be modest, yet committed. You'd be surprised how many writers are willing to write a small check. And small checks matter. The presses need to have the same persistence in the face of rejection as a writer does. Presses also need to think about doing group fund-raising. And that won't be easy; the literary world is notoriously and appropriately individualized."

Individuals have been the mainstays of small press publishing, and some of them—with the late James Laughlin of New Directions as perhaps the classic example—have also exerted a significant influence on the funding of poetry publishing. As Michael Anania sees it, "If Laughlin's family hadn't put up with his depletion of the family fortune to publish New Directions poetry, we wouldn't *have* the poetry of modernism. We all think of New Directions now as a cultural institution, but as late as the 1960s it was still a small press." Other such "institutions" might include the Ecco Press and Black Sparrow Press.

Among those individuals recently entering the field was the anonymous donor who endowed the Eric Mathieu King Fund at the Academy of American Poets in 1995. The King Fund supports poetry book publishing. Another anonymous benefactor made possible the establishment in 1994 of Sarabande Books in

Louisville, Kentucky, after its founders—all writers themselves, led by poets Sarah Gorham and Jeffrey Skinner—had been laying plans independently. Nearly one-third of Story Line Press's budget two years ago had its origins in private donations, attributed in part to the press's active national board of directors. Robert McDowell, director of the fourteen-year-old Oregon press, "relies on my board to search for angels. As the staff, you're too busy staggering along and publishing to do fund-raising."

Martha Rhodes, who with Dzvinia Orlowsky began Four Way Books in 1992 to publish poetry books primarily, agrees with McDowell about the need for assistance with fund-raising. "I can sometimes be too passionate about my press," she sighs. "I'd like to be accompanied by a seasoned fund-raiser in my pitch. Otherwise, I might come across as too much of a puppy dog who doesn't want to be leashed."

Traditionally poetry has always been "funded," to some degree, by you and me following our noses in various bookshops. Paul Yamazaki, the buyer at San Francisco's City Lights bookstore, feels fairly sanguine about the commerce of poetry. "One of the first things people think of when they think of City Lights is poetry," he acknowledges. "We have that unique advantage." Even so, it's encouraging to learn that poetry sales at City Lights in 1995–96 constituted 8½ percent of total store revenues, up from 2 percent ten years earlier. In the two years since 1996, poetry revenues at City Lights have again risen; they now comprise 9 percent of total store sales. Yamazaki notes a 100 percent increase in hardcover poetry sales alone.

Store space for poetry has quadrupled over the last dozen years; both change and growth are obvious in the City Lights clientele. "We are seeing two major audiences," Yamazaki says, "baby boomers returning to poetry (their tastes tend to be conservative) and a generation of readers in their twenties and younger who are coming to poetry for the first time in large numbers. Formally and stylistically, demand is all over the map. As there are many different ways of writing poetry, there are many different ways of buying it. The interest in poetry is a very solid thing, not a short surge," he promises.

As evidence of that interest, Yamazaki mentions the success in his store of poetry books published by the smallest of the small presses and sent his way through the good graces of the literary wholesaler Small Press Distribution. "The sell-through rate for Small Press Distribution books is close to 100 percent, and they are books we offer only in ones or twos, with very little publicity. Yet there is an audience for them."

John Marshall and Christine Deavel own and operate a poetry-only bookstore in Seattle that is apparently one of just two in the country. Open Books: A Poem Emporium became a pragmatic possibility after Marshall, himself a poet, had tracked poetry sales in his previous store, a general-interest independent in the same university neighborhood, over a long period and found that his poetry and prose about poetry had expanded to 50 percent of his sales and 40 percent of his stock. From Marshall's perspective, a poetry-only store is in fact less risky than a general independent, partly because chains and superstores are unable to compete with the depth of his current poetry stock. (In fact, the chains in Seattle increasingly refer their poetry customers to him.) The average purchase per customer in his store in 1996: 1.9 books, versus 1.2 in the previous general-interest shop. By April of 1998, that figure rose to an average of more than two books purchased per customer.

"People have come to trust us," he comments in 1998. "This store is a mom-and-pop, and so we stock our own taste. In our store, small press books are doing very well as compared with poetry books put out by other sorts of publishers. The big houses seem to be doing less with poetry. The quirkier poetry is handled by small presses. Either the audience for that kind of poetry is growing, or they're finding us more readily." The store's taste also seems to be contagious. "Business is up this year 15 or 20 percent," Marshall reports, and part of it comes from out-of-state customers who drop in every now and then or place orders from afar. In effect, these customers are like bookstore subscribers. The store's active mailing list now numbers 600 names.

The two books sold on average to every customer at Open Books may well include an eighth or a third of a title published under Sun & Moon's nonprofit aegis. Sun & Moon publisher and director Douglas Messerli sounds exultant when he reports, "Poetry books are among our best-selling titles." Though his company has received outside funding from time to time, "we are actually surviving on sales now," he says.

Sun & Moon got started in Los Angeles in 1976 when Messerli, then a college professor, left the academic life. In 1995, with a staff of three, Sun & Moon produced seventy-nine titles, half of them poetry. Thirty percent of overall book sales are classroom-related. Messerli credits this figure to his list's concentration on "innovative" and avant-garde poetry, as well as fiction. "Poetry that is more serious-minded or more 'difficult' will be more attractive to the university audience."

His list shrank to forty books in 1996 (with half of them poetry), to thirty in 1997 (with a third of those poetry), and returned to forty again in 1998 (with three-quarters poetry). Messerli holds Sun &

Moon's losses in grant funding responsible for the declining numbers; he points to Mellon funding as the driving force behind the seventy-nine-book list in 1995. "We still don't understand how we managed to publish seventy-nine, which is more than a book a week," he laughs. "Forty is much more than most literary lists, especially with a three-person staff. We worked just as hard on forty as we did on seventy-nine." He seconds Thom Ward's advice to pursue foreign and reprint rights sales as an increasingly important source of income for small presses that have had the funding rug pulled out from under them. And Messerli has also looked to foreign governments as funders for appropriate titles, especially as his press's focus gradually moves from American literature to international writing. He notes a 10 percent increase in sales for Sun & Moon in 1996–97.

As sales-driven as Messerli, but with a totally different approach to poetry publishing, is Gary Hustwit, who launched Incommunicado Press in 1994 in association with his existing company, Rockpress Publishing, which specializes in music reference titles. "We're for-profit, definitely! We've never applied for a grant or solicited donations," avers Hustwit. "If you can't support yourself on your own, then you shouldn't be doing it. Low overhead is key, and selling a lot of mail order and at readings."

Incommunicado also releases novels and short fiction, but to poetry readers it is well known for an emphasis on spoken-word poetry by twenty-something Los Angeles writers. "Our music interest bleeds into performance poetry," concedes the San Diego-based publisher. "But there are no preconceived boundaries as categories. Our books are a collage of different viewpoints." And they are, incidentally, reaching a hotly desired audience—what Hustwit scoffingly calls "the prefab plot" of Generation X.

"Until recently," he observes, "no books were being published for the younger spoken-word audience. I don't think it's that they don't want to read. But they won't flip through just any poetry book and buy it. And this audience probably won't respond to a corporate publisher's typical sales pitch." Since most of Incommunicado's authors are also rock musicians or performers, they "tour" routinely under their own steam to a network of venues unknown to many poets—bars, clubs, and underground spots whose audiences are not there for the love of poesy, but who may learn to love it.

Known as a marketing whiz, literary agent Ira Silverberg was previously associate publisher of Serpent's Tail/High Risk Books, where he served "the needs of a nontraditional poetry community. We worked with poets—June Jordan, Sapphire, David Trinidad— who do not fit into *The New Yorker*." Though Serpent's Tail/High Risk published no more than one poetry book each season, he chose to publish one "so there'd be no competition. We weren't competing with ourselves."

Silverberg wastes no words in explaining why he did as he did. "Poetry does require special marketing strategies," he insists, "but these are particular to titles and authors, not to the genre as a whole. Marketing poetry is a title-by-title endeavor. Small presses can promote poetry far better than large houses because each poetry title is central to the list. A poetry book could have been our lead title at Serpent's Tail. Unfortunately, trade house poetry tends to get more widely reviewed—but small press poetry ultimately sells better in bookstores."

Another for-profit small independent publisher, Moyer Bell, contends regularly with poetry on its list. "My job as a publisher," says Jennifer Moyer, "is to sell my books. I don't think 'sales' is a dirty word; I think it's a sweet one. To stay in business, I have to publish a balance of books, and get people revved up about them—battle the attitude, 'Oh dear, here comes another nonselling literary title from Moyer Bell.' And there's a finite number of sales that one can make in poetry. I'm constantly taking money out of the bank to pay for these poetry books, and I never get the money back. I have to renew the justification, or I'll resent it. Bookstores in general have been less willing to set aside precious shelf space to slow-selling titles like poetry. Poetry contributes as much—or as little—to a bookstore's bottom line as to a publisher's. Stores are buying fewer poetry titles and in smaller quantities. And if the store does not have the books on the shelf, they won't get bought."

What ultimately sells a book of poetry, believes Randy Blasing, the editor of Copper Beech Press in Providence, Rhode Island, "is word of mouth. All the distribution and advertising in the world won't matter. Presence in a bookstore doesn't mean it will sell. Every day our voice mail has at least ten messages from people—strangers—wanting to order books. It's mysterious." Nevertheless, warns Blasing, who has been in business since 1983, "we don't know what success is, because success in America is money—and we don't make any. When we publish something, we take it out of our own hides. We're saying, this is worth our time, our lives."

That may be the common lot of most small press publishers of poetry. Edwin Frank, cofounder of Alef Books in New York, entered poetry book publishing in 1993 as a newcomer. "We imagined it might be a quixotic effort, but there has been more payback and response than we envisioned," he says. "Organization is a constant problem when you have only two people working part-time to publish books and get grant money. But small presses are often a labor of love. Those presses that struggle through will be *more* appreciated."

## The Small Press Muse and Its Difficulties

The panorama from the desk of a poetry critic can be shrouded, at times, in the mists of literary fashion, failure, and perversity. But "the scene for poetry would be a very grim one without the small presses," agrees Herb Leibowitz, editor and publisher of the journal *Parnassus: Poetry in Review.* "Small presses all over the poetry landscape are doing all kinds of archaeological digging. Each small press has to find its own passions and bring them to people. Sharpen your nails, so you can cling to the cliff!"

What other kinds of tests or challenges should be faced by small press poetry publishers? Inevitably, the necessary passage of leadership from founding publisher to inheritor. In time, the recognition or reaffirmation of a press's niche or character. Also, the rebirth of defiance as a publishing strategy; though not often talked about, it is essential. Continually, the reinvention of the publishing company by its writers, who should contest its identity. And partly, the evolution of closer, more cooperative relationships with other small presses and independent counterparts, such as bookstores. All this in addition to redoubled efforts in marketing, sales, and fund-raising.

But publishing—any kind of publishing—is largely the business of opinion. Mine and yours.

# Poets Are Not a Special Breed:
# Galway Kinnell

THE LOWER EAST SIDE is said to be gentrifying. But an early-morning exploration of New York suggests otherwise. Garbage and gewgaws of the street shift on curbs. Flecks stray in the air like sleazy sprites. The rumbling art of trucks is spelled out. In the absence of people, objects assume a humanity that may be better than ours. All the leftovers of Manhattan—bleary neon, blooming graffiti—seem ridden with life, like an attractive substitute for nature.

The poet Galway Kinnell, who lived in this urban neighborhood as a younger man, has since exchanged it for an upper-story high-rise apartment in a Greenwich Village complex. But his glassed-in view evokes the promise offered up by all cities, especially this one: an unlimited capacity for hope *and* garbage.

One is fortunate to find Kinnell momentarily afloat here. Vermont's former poet laureate spends much of his time at home in a farmhouse or traveling far and wide for poetry. At sixty-seven, the Pulitzer prize–winning writer is pausing for Houghton Mifflin's publication of *Imperfect Thirst* (1994), his twelfth collection.

In Kinnell's poetry, such places as the Lower East Side appear as if glimpsed through a mythic magnifying glass, and the poet has lowered the same intent instrument to seek out the substance of pigpens and meadows, as well as turning it directly on his own life. His point seems not to be describing or illustrating facts of nature, human or inhuman, but summoning their essence, with lyric violence or tenderness, and confirming a kinship.

"Writing a poem is like making an artifact," Kinnell explains. "It is making something physical out of words. There is a wholeness to a poem, as with a vase. There is also a sense of talking to someone, the reader.

"But we all have such different ideas of what poetry is. To me, poetry is somebody standing up, so to speak, and saying, with as little concealment as possible, what it is for him or her to be on earth at this moment. In no other art can we do that directly in words. That may be why so many people are writing poetry. They want to say what it is for them to live now. Poets are not, as they used to be, a special breed, set apart."

Born in Providence, Rhode Island, and educated at Princeton University and the University of Rochester, Kinnell was first a reader of poetry who did not suspect he was a poet. But he considered himself "different from other people, because I lived a solitary life, and everything that mattered to me happened within me," he says. "The emotion that I felt most strongly during childhood and which I never spoke about was loneliness. It might be the *only* emotion that I felt. It was so strong that it erased all the others.

"My relationships with other people were—well, I won't say they weren't deep, but they were almost without words. 'Has the cat got his tongue?' was a question I would hear over and over. I had a kind of muteness as a child. When I began to read poetry at around fourteen, it was thrilling to me to find poets who were talking about the things that really mattered to me. I became very attached to poetry."

Kinnell credits his Princeton teacher Charles G. Bell as an important source of encouragement for a young poet who "lacked confidence. I was steeped in poetry before I began to write, and the tradition in which I wrote used a lot of conventional symbols and expressed a lot of conventionally poetic feelings about the world, so that my poems hardly touched any of my real feelings for many years. I gradually learned that poetry of that sort, while it offered an opportunity to express things, also had the effect of hiding them, and I had to rid myself of the conventions of poetry before I *could* express those things. Yet I also had to keep what was true about that kind of poetry.

"There is a tendency in one poetic tradition toward inflation of feeling and inflation of language, toward using words that have accumulated a lot of emotion through their use in other poems before you, so that when you use them, you mistakenly think you're expressing something of your own."

As well as trying to shed this habit, the young Kinnell decided to abandon rhyme and meter. "This wasn't so much because they were conventional, but because I found it difficult to concentrate on what I was saying while I was thinking about rhyme and meter," he reflects. "I worked so hard at my rhymes because they didn't come naturally to me—and neither did meter. I wanted the rhymes to come within the lines, and not in a regular pattern. And I wanted an imitative music, rather than a metric or counted one.

"I don't mean that counted meter may not be imitative. In the hands of the great practitioners, it often is. But I found it difficult. My turning away from rhyme and meter had as much to do with my own limitations as with my judgments about rhyme and meter."

Kinnell's first collection of poetry, *What a Kingdom It Was*, was published by Houghton Mifflin in 1960, though his first book-length work, as a translator, actually preceded this: the poet's version of Rene Hardy's *Bitter Victory* was issued by Doubleday in 1956. (Kinnell has become especially noted for his translations of Francois Villon and Yves Bonnefoy.) A single novel, *Black Light*, was published by Houghton in 1966 and reissued in a revised edition by North Point Press in 1980. His children's book, *How the Alligator Missed Breakfast*, came from Houghton in 1982. Except for occasional excursions into small press publishing and one book issued by Knopf, Kinnell has seen most of his work put out by Houghton, from *Flower Herding on Mount Monadnock* (1964) through *Three Books* (1993), which collected in revised form the poetry of three earlier books, *Body Rags* (1968), *Mortal Acts, Mortal Words* (1980), and *The Past* (1985). His editors at the house have included the late George Starbuck, Jonathan Galassi, Nan Talese, and Peter Davison, the editor of *Imperfect Thirst*.

Starbuck, his first editor, remembered the poet not only as a writer but also as a teacher—"a teacher with a capital 'T.'" Kinnell ran an adult education program at the University of Chicago from 1951 to 1955 while Starbuck, also a poet, was a Chicago graduate student before entering publishing. "He was a brilliant, dedicated teacher," Starbuck says. "It was his vocation. I can remember hearing a couple of the older graduate students wondering whether Robert Maynard Hutchins might have had the same kind of sexiness and bemusement as Galway had."

Kinnell has since taught in France and Iran, as well as at Sarah

Lawrence College, the University of Iowa, Columbia University, and elsewhere in this country. He was the first director of the creative writing program at New York University. At a recent New York City reading by poet Jane Cooper, sponsored by Poets House, Kinnell recalled his debt to Cooper as a teacher when both taught at Sarah Lawrence. "I was impressed by the amount of time and patience and affection she bestowed upon her students," he says. His own method, developed over the years: use class time as an opportunity to build "a completely welcoming place for poetry where students are nevertheless competing in a friendly way"; use office hours for more intensive and particular textual and critical labors. At a time when the teaching of writing is widespread and yet not always appreciated either by educators or students, outsiders or insiders, the method has stood Kinnell in good stead.

Fellow writers have helped Kinnell as teachers, and they have also served him well as editors. He relies on them for guidance in his own work. "I show my poems to friends not just because I like to show them, but because I need help," he says. "The person I've shown my poems to for most of my writing life has been my teacher, Charles G. Bell. But Philip Levine, Hayden Carruth, Donald Hall, and Robert Bly have also been people with whom I've exchanged poems for a long time. In recent years, Sharon Olds has been the one I've counted on most.

"I count on them all for whatever suggestions they might have. I can't tell them, 'I need you to help me do *x* and *y*'; I just send them the poems and say, 'I'm not sure if I can ever finish this poem. Do you have any thoughts on that?' Robert Bly always tends to say, 'Well, it's too long. Stop it here.' We used to say jokingly of him that if Homer had sent him the *Iliad*, he would have turned it into a haiku.

"What I hope for from my writer friends is some sense of whether a poem can become a poem or not. There's a point at which I will have worked and worked and worked on the poem, and it still doesn't seem to be near to being a poem. And sometimes they might encourage me to keep going, and sometimes, on the contrary, they might say, 'Actually, it looks hopeless.' They also help me on deeper matters of truthfulness and accuracy with respect to the emotions—Sharon's very good at that." Olds also teaches at NYU.

Kinnell is a dedicated reviser of his poetry, making extensive changes for as long as time allows in a book's production process: "I am a slow writer."

⨳

ALTHOUGH IT'S DANGEROUS to venture general statements about contemporary poetry, it would seem that in the United States poetry has been democratized in this century: more people are writing it, whether "professionally" or not. One of the forces behind the change was Walt Whitman, and another at work on it is Galway Kinnell, whose writing life was altered by his reading of Whitman. "I still feel that I am a son of Whitman. But Whitman is no longer that perfect father to me," he says, with some relish. "I think that as you get to know poets' work better, and the poets through their work, you see there are things that they couldn't do, and in a way, you love them more, because for the first time they are not gods but humans.

"I feel a certain kinship with some New England writers, like Thoreau and Frost," Kinnell observes. "But I don't like the closed self of the Puritan ethos. Soon Whitman became more important to me than any of the New England poets except Dickinson, because he wanted to be able to say everything. A little later, Dickinson became just as important to me. I understood that she, too, wanted to say everything: she said more about the emotional life than any other poet."

Why is it necessary for a poet to want to say "everything"? Because, replies Kinnell, "We have a lot of inhibitions about emotions that are thought to be shameful and private and unspeakable. But to reach another person, poetry has to be as open as possible. Then we discover that everyone's experience resembles everyone else's."

Kinnell's writing life seems to have consisted of a gradual unfolding, a gradual loss of concealment. And his experience as a public reader of his poetry may have run parallel to that.

A reading by Kinnell suggests a little of both god and human. When he and Allen Ginsberg shared the stage at New York City's St. Mark's Church in the spring of 1993, for example, Ginsberg sang and chanted with the harum-scarum zealotry of an irresistible Sufi mensch. Kinnell, on the other hand, wearing his signature white linen suit, seemed a courtly shaman, reading aloud with great eloquence a poem from *Imperfect Thirst* called "Holy Shit."

"Poetry is useful," he says. "Poetry can help us to feel more attuned to what's real—to feel more a part of the rhythms of life. Every poem in some way chronicles an aspect of human life...it makes us less estranged from the earth. It makes us feel that we belong here: we're mortal earthlings, we're animals."

SAINT FRANCIS AND THE SOW
*by Galway Kinnell*

The bud
stands for all things,
even for those things that don't flower,

for everything flowers, from within, of self-blessing;
though sometimes it is necessary
to reteach a thing its loveliness,
to put a hand on its brow
of the flower
and retell it in words and in touch
it is lovely
until it flowers again from within, of self-blessing;
as Saint Francis
put his hand on the creased forehead
of the sow, and told her in words and in touch
blessings of earth on the sow, and the sow
began remembering all down her thick length,
from the earthen snout all the way
through the fodder and slops to the spiritual curl of the tail,
from the hard spininess spiked out from the spine
down through the great broken heart
to the sheer blue milken dreaminess spurting and shuddering
from the fourteen teats into the fourteen mouths sucking and
    blowing beneath them:
the long, perfect loveliness of sow.

# Mortal Immortal

FOR MONTHS ON END, THE INSCAPES and landscapes of Georgia O'Keeffe's flower paintings wait for me as if at the other end of a spyglass. I draw nearer and beam in, feeling guilty about my prurient curiosity, the imperfect, frustrated understanding that leads to my preoccupation with her and to my sundry fits of tourism. Her paintings tempt me, like exotica, with an unfamiliar temperament. I don't yet have the words for them.

Every flower, though, suggests to me a perplexing architecture of retreats and expanses. I prefer to watch the ebbings and the boundaries in the paintings, not their hardy points of avowal. O'Keeffe seems to have reserved her finest strokes for the former. They are finest in the sense of being most fulfilled, most accurate. For example, in *White Rose No. 2* (1927), the unevenly concentric, abstract seraph of the pale, ash-stroked flower seems lunar and conjured, like a dune about to dissolve. The white-on-white stillnesses at the core are just barely absolved of all license to own hue. It seems strange to be able to decipher their bleached voluptuousness, but by wondering for long enough, you can. A swirly intransigence yields at the flower's outer swathes and rings to the definite dark diagonals that sanction and concretize the silence permeating the picture. For something that is so complex and complete, the rose seems oddly effervescent, disembodied of the burden to expose itself, fact by fact. This flower resembles many other things besides a flower: a bodily tissue, an eddy, a terrain, a "thought." By magnifying the rose's size and scope, O'Keeffe restored the flower as a symbol. But she also chose to let a flower be no less than it utterly was, a mortal immortal.

Some flowers seem more mortal than others. In the body of *Black Iris II* (1936), the flutter of the typical iris headpiece is recognizable, even literal in spirit. Still, this iris seems overtaken by a motive foreign to itself, by a shiver, of dismay or delight. The opening at the center is a dark, slack question caught in the middle of its life, uncertain of what the iris should be, other than a question—an aghast question bottled in the gesture, at that.

O'Keeffe is well known for the confidence of her floral raptures, and *Purple Petunia* (1927) unlooses some of those. The actressy, plush waves of reddening plum color in the supple petal-paths evoke opera-house curtains, warming with unseen sound. The flower is nearly personified, like a ballyhooed soprano arching toward her prime in the surge of a glorious yet limited career. We can imagine the anticlimax and the end, the wilt, the necessary floundering to come. But the dimples and the bounds of the petals are also idiosyncratic, earthly, unoperatic. They seem improvised as a touch, without known cause; momentarily themselves, and not about to have second thoughts.

Her fullness of view seems artless and more truthful than a documentary conscience could be, less constrained by human vanity than many other painters have been. I wake to O'Keeffe's unself-conscious flower glimpses as though believing for the first time that nothing can obstruct the way between ourselves and nature.

And I wake to find the elated fury in *Red Canna* (1924), a formal envelopment of flames, plumes, and tinted upward trails. Vertically relaxing streams tip aloft, not in a hurry. One can't personify or patronize the little curving, bubbly band of carnelian-color that ripples on the right, meandering awhile. You'd like to know where the flower's central vee—its cusp, its rise—has ascended from, and just how all the efflorescence enwrapping it began. But the eye can't know all, O'Keeffe's did not, and her limits are intrinsic to her expansive knack. She doesn't explain, will not moralize. The paintings are only as subtle as the flowers, without the seeming imposition of an artist's—or a human's—demands for submission or challenge.

When she slips from skill, the pictures lose clarity, lack imaginative belief. In *Pink Tulip* (1926) the pistil cameo embedded in the portrait has been generalized—this self isn't really attached to the flower housing it; it's residential noncommittally, an artist's oversight. Maybe she tired of the obviousness of the pistil role and the organ's pose. Her attention seems to have wandered to the outer folds of petal, which darken toward an edge whose drama is more inherent and instantly more fetching: the movement of the line in its unseeking, untrammeled progress.

Another slip of O'Keeffe's, occasional and yet characteristic: sentimentality in color and composition. You can find it in the puffed-sleeve, birthday-girl soft tone of *Blue Flower* (1924–28) or in the stage-managed dewdrop of *Black Petunia & White Morning-Glory I* (1926), teetering unpersuasively on the black petal. Her view of larkspur in *White Rose with Larkspur No. 1 and No. 2* (1927) seems less fraught and less decided than larkspur really is. Her *White Pansy* (1927), with those tiny forget-me-nots encircling the Betty Boop–like, winsome face of the pansy, seems jokily fey, a mild-mannered snapshot. Yet flowers too have their etiquette and their dauphines, and perhaps the lesser O'Keeffe was simply bowing, with amusement, to the cuter archangels of the parade.

For me her best work shows the drama of clarity emerging invincibly, as though in involuntary error, and gradually coming to command nature, routing the crowd of customary faces and feelings, and suggesting a less personal, more cosmic relation by hue and scale alone. Her more abstract floral views may have been pursued as though they, too, were factually true — an enchanting thought, revealing faith in the imagining eye as in the object. The sureness of her abstractions brings serenity and Dickinsonian intimations of huge, unforeseen spaces in the mortal.

O'Keeffe's jack-in-the-pulpit series is the most Dickinsonian example, telling of the crackle of emergence from a blackened, wiry, underfoot flower that seems to haggle in the shadow for ascendancy, surrounded by greenish, rhythmic turbulence. Coded as a papal emissary, wrapped in pride, the mannish flower struts up horselike with grandeur in the first two paintings of the series. But by the third, fourth, fifth, and sixth, the dominating spirit of a personage has begun to subside, as though a crack burst and something more like truth, less like earth, claimed a place on the canvas. The thin white flare in number four juts simply from the dark blue pulse; the entire form has gone ribbony, struck, a full sheath beaten in blue monument. The scale of liberated innerness swells the scene in number five, as abstracted momentum seizes a current and whirls. (The icy flare has turned narrow and crimson here, more essential, less mere.) And in number six, O'Keeffe finally spectralizes the flower, lowering her gaze on the innermost part and revealing this solemnly, as if it were a feudal wand, a dusky firework.

The jack-in-the-pulpit series implies a transformation of flower into metaphor without any explication. For me, the meaning of the metaphor remains uncertain, as new and severe as the flower. I can think of no way to justify O'Keeffe's flowers, just as there is no way to account fully for nature's casting choices and changes. (Science's questions, answers, and summaries will not do, for now.) Her refusal to document and her decision not to portray herself cause my muddle, in part. But it's a muddle I can't do without.

Just out of his teens, the poet Rilke confessed to his diary: "Tired of art, one seeks the artist, and in each work looks for the deed that edified the man, the triumph over something within him, and the longing for himself." Even so, Rilke decided, "In peak times of art a few have erected before themselves, in addition to their own beauty, so much noble heritage, that the work no longer needs them."

On a drizzly August morning, the peremptory madonna-blue of clambering morning glories is saturated suddenly with water droplets. The rain splatters the flower with dashing pink streams. This fresh ink at first seems inappropriate to the morning glory's scheme. But however the sultry splashes came to be, they're true to the flower now. The author is invisible, and the picture stuns.

# Bookless

To be without your books for longer than a chance few weeks is like squandering your mind, of your own free will. You have given it away, along with Seamus Heaney's last several volumes and *Absalom, Absalom!*, Arthur Conan Doyle and *The Duino Elegies*. If the books were deliberately alphabetized, sorted by genre, hurried off their shelves, boxed, sealed, and driven to a rambling storage warehouse in a town without a name, then their former owner has succeeded in darkening a room of herself. Nothing can make the perversion come right again. And yet, there was nowhere else to put them.

I was sick and didn't know it for about five years. The illness was undermining but not dramatic till near the end. Before then, I always supposed that I was merely tired, tired like a Kafka character who mopes and toils redundantly, symbolically—unrelieved, unrewarded, unnoticed. Appropriately for the plot of my story, I had a symbol for my malaise: it was the book. I toiled and sickened over books partly because I was a book review editor at a magazine.

Mounds of books rose and fell every day at the office, arriving in padded brown envelopes both innocuous and alluring. Like the fading urban sprite from Kafka, I was comforted by their plausible yet sometimes bogus bulk, which was bedlike. All too often, mere palaver plumped inside the envelopes—stacks of words like stacks of books. To my nose there sometimes flew the aroma of beefsteak from pages like perfume. A few demure volumes with pudgy trim sizes were being marketed, it seemed, as good luck charms, or as coasters. Others were fat with commercial fantasies and formulas. Easier to miss were the literary gems and hoaxes, poorly dressed for the part. I slept standing up while bending down to unstaple the envelopes; I strained small tendons, lugging galleys around. I organized in cubicleville the praise and disapprovals of the paragraph scribes, our freelance reviewers. I myself was a paragraph scribe. I listened frequently to the book publicists, for whom listening can be an unaccustomed, unacknowledged art.

But an "I" is just a myth to the bacterial invader. When attacked, the self must try to protect its own singular chaos. Yet if you're sick, you really can't. Dolled up with germs and flattered by their revelry, I received their daily salutes until my health finally broke. Then, abruptly arthritic, I couldn't walk. I may have loved the books and left the job because neither could finally do right by my chaos.

☒

YET FIRST I SWAM IN BOOKS; I swam in sickness. I was dizzy, dry in the mouth, itchy under the skin. I read for pleasure, I read for redemption, indiscriminately, obediently. I became thin and thinner. There was no time for lunch. I was wearing out too fast to keep track. I swayed, counted, sighed, husbanding the new titles as they arrived on my carnivorous-maroon aluminum office shelf: books to be reviewed by others; books to be reviewed by me; books to be held, for now; others, to be tossed. The building blocks of any house of employment were rarely more lovely or more oppressive.

Meanwhile, I was fortifying my domestic kingdom, dragging home the books the office didn't want. I had found a big apartment after a year's search for wall space and other amenities. There I painted bookcase after bookcase white, not carnivorous. I also secreted a stash of books at the end of my top-floor hallway: boxes and boxes of shiny new books rising splendidly near the exit to the roof. Of course, this was a fire hazard, but no fire was expected. My books held up the house, didn't they? Brash and tactile, with something important to impart? Late at night, I would crouch in the hall, exhausted, and bemused by all my books, turning pages but not reading. They were my soul's money.

THERE WAS ROOM ENOUGH AT HOME to keep my path free of books, but I preferred instead to fill it, endow it. So the books of my favorite authors were piled up neatly in nightly varying arrangements on the floor, beside the rivalrous furniture. I especially liked to watch what the lamplight could make of my exhibits: a dull red cover grew burnished, replete, English; another book jacket's spiky minimalism swelled into its own, like a glittering mollusk. The mornings found us all glum, reluctantly prepared to wait out the long daylight hours until another bibliomaniacal performance would charm us.

I was dumb before books, good or bad, promising or plainly trash. They were my companions. They told me what they could, and they didn't demand much investigative energy from me. They were sympathetic to my lot. A recurrent flu, which my doctor seemed unable to rid me of, often left me cryptic and perplexed. I took medical tests, but they revealed nothing. I gradually grew much too depleted to say more to anyone than was expressly needed. A friend in Texas phoned and suggested to me humorously, "You sound like Dostoyevsky."

☒

AN EXPLANATION FOR MY MALAISE: someplace on Tick Lane in the woods, I had actually been bitten long ago by a denizen bug and furtively given Lyme disease, a "minor" but often chronic ailment for which the diagnostic tools are inexact, the cure elusive. Symptoms and treatments vary. But I regard Lyme disease now mostly as a book disease because of how it tested my loyalties. I had to fail the test; there was no alternative.

Finally diagnosed but physically compromised, lacking a job, though offered another, with my father very recently dead, and my body and my feelings unforgivingly inflamed, I decided to move out of my apartment. To do it to the nth, I packed up almost everything and put it into storage. Especially the books, my glowing metaphysical furniture. I did the work carefully. Libraries around the state became my buddy beneficiaries for a few hundred volumes. Other people had their literary loans at last returned to them. But that still left me with an impressive hoard of titles, none of which I have seen in several years. They remain in storage.

It worries me, this temporary loss prolonged until my old

courtship and ownership of books seems only a fantasy, nothing to count on. Like an ex who doesn't want to be reminded, I avoid the chummy clamor of the bookstores. Libraries are serene and evocative, like crowded crypts with rapt, distorted figures elaborately preserved in the cold, formal light. Their returned gaze feels glassy, with a buried motive.

The professional business I've continued to conduct with books seems somewhat otherworldly to me. I have become bookless.

# Address Book

WHEN PEOPLE PREFER TO RIFFLE THROUGH their Rolodexes, Filofaxes, and electronic reference bins, the address book is supposed to be a thing of the past. I'm fond of my address books, though, keep several, and also resent them because they are old and shambling, precarious heaps that have lasted all the same. They shake like bugs in the ground, their papery orbs dangling.

My most senior address book is no longer extant and thus difficult to recall, but dark green, with gold lettering, very small. My newest is shiny, narrow, and orange, made in Finland and found at a dull moment in a friend's basement. Not very practical, but easy to bring to hand. My main address book is neither of those—square, red, dingy, and crammed with wrinkled addenda, such as the home phone number of the unhappy uptown book marketing manager who had decided to move back to Minnesota, away from his awful boss. (I picture him cheery-eyed and exhilarant now at minus twenty, his native *ressentiment* thrillingly compounded by the blameless lick of frost.) The memento he left to me is just an angular scrawl from another (yet another) hapless afternoon of his angst in publishing, which I happened to interrupt.

Some address-book souvenirs are strikingly visual, unlike his. In one of mine that demands to be ogled, a princess, nameless, gazes up from her tellingly discreet photographic portrait on her business card, which provides a phone number and nothing more by way of word. Her hair looks priceless—smooth, brown, furled. Etched in by a wand, her elfin eyes and swanky nose must have appealed rather strongly to the magazine editor whose nook I was visiting and ransacking a few years ago. He was very late for our appointment and had left no message for me in his absence, so I restlessly went looking for something nice to read. But he didn't keep any books close by—the corporation wouldn't have liked it. Hemmed in by hanging files and selfless paraphernalia, all congealing together under the fluorescence, I snatched the first toy I could and slipped it into my address book, which was handy. As booty, it wasn't bad. Now I knew what Billy really had on his mind. I'll call her Lynelle.

My address book is a symptom of my enervation, a totem of rushed days, past and to come. Yet not everyone's is like that. I have seen martial, puritan address books, for instance, listing people who have not once switched their jobs or addresses; they will never leave town or die. The squadrons of these lucky listed ones are chaperoned through the years by their friend, who owns the saintly address book. Writing myself into those tombs, upon request, has always struck me as morbid, a polite form of interment.

To read my red address book is almost as beleaguering as to compile it. Both are unrewarding activities. The address book, by now, isn't meant to be read, or even skimmed. Instead it's a small harbor for detritus, for floating names without secondary sex characteristics. The density of expired or expiring persons (associates come and go, too feckless to be friends) gets in the way of finding anyone who might still be current. I could tidy the mess by inking the expatriates and forgettables. Yet I'm charitable—I don't want to cross people out just because they haven't called or written me in years. Let them eliminate themselves, at their leisure. I should simply write a new address book, I suppose.

That writing assignment is different from any other, a delicate exercise in damning autobiography and a giddy revel in biblio-mania, if one's book is one's life. I doubt I will do it soon. But I enjoy imagining a new address book for myself as an ideal object symbolically invested with the dignity of all the kindred address books that have humbly, numbly cluttered human satchels and desk drawers over time. Mine would be a perfect thing—and no, I will never achieve it, never own it. But I can believe anyway in the ideal address book.

This address book of the future will be very thick, but not very heavy. The order of its pages can be altered at will, and new ones added on whenever I need more. The categories and subdivisions, likewise, can shift, the alphabet be dashed, with expirees shuttled to the back and certain people grouped professionally or geographically (or both). A hobby can occupy a chapter of its own and be dismantled when my interest dwindles and I'm no longer calling those numbers. It will be possible to erase and replace or emend any item. You can do everything with a pen, not a mouse. There will be room for annotations: com-ments recording my first impressions of a person, qualified by more recent thoughts; rotating nicknames; reminders to call someone once a year, just for the sake of it. Waterproofing of paper and pen means no confusion coming up. A fat hold-all toward the rear can house miscel-laneous information, to be discarded at a whim: book titles and poems lately discovered, safe combinations, and 800 numbers.

There will also be a home in the ideal address book for impromptu, impractical bits of fantasy and nostalgia—like the long-out-of-date Hoboken street name and apartment number of a friend who later went to Tennessee, then to Louisiana, and next to total silence. Her silence will not be solved, probably. She wouldn't like it to be solved. But somewhere she's sitting in a tumbledown chair, regretting the humidity. I never knew her well—at most, three conversations linked us, and a thin assortment of other shared experiences, poetry among those. Jane is like many inhabitants of my address book: hastily written into it, but with a verifying ruggedness of stroke.

A catalogue of inconstancy and a never-ending novel, my address book is less attractive than the carved and beaten records in stone of the ancients, which stand vertically preserved. There is something poetic and fatal, by comparison, about the way my people drift and hide. Even my classic stalwarts, the addressees who've mostly stayed put, or who have moved ahead and kept me up to date, seem like orphaned line items, sometimes.

To write a new address book could require a new handwriting as well as a fresh pen, and a different kind of author. It might need to include a lot of extra blank space—room to embroider, analyze, and absolve my various characters of their collective misfortunes. Searching recently like a soothsayer through my red address book, I found illnesses, deaths, acrimony, complacence, weary or unidentifiable entries. (Who *is* Sharene Z. Walsh?) I may have friends whom I can't remember. If that is so, then I may as well invent some others, for the entertainment of the writing and the worth of the book itself.

Who can say that I don't have F. Scott Fitzgerald's fax number? Or that I've never given him a call?

# Harriet's Ghost

IN 1912, WHEN SHE WAS FIFTY-ONE, Harriet Monroe founded *Poetry* magazine. Her personal papers and those of the magazine are kept at the University of Chicago in a series of files stacked in elegant, slate-colored tombstone boxes. It is peaceful to open them, hoping to catch a glimpse of Harriet's ghost. Along with hers linger phantoms of colleagues and correspondents from Vachel Lindsay to Ezra Pound.

Probably Monroe interests me more than I would interest her. I especially like her unflamboyant urge to publish a journal of poetry every month in a city better known for trains and meat than verse. It would have been easier not to do this, not to magnetize the social and artistic circles she chose. For unlike Margaret Anderson, her editorial rival and fellow midwesterner who edited the *Little Review*, Monroe wasn't born to be a bohemian, and never became one. She didn't *want* to camp out on Lake Michigan during the summers; she was a lawyer's daughter, and needed a house. "Those breakfasts of ham and eggs, or chops and potatoes, with hot rolls or steaming piles of buckwheat cakes!" Monroe reminisced in her memoirs about her childhood's repasts. "Those dinners, with a roast or steak or perhaps game birds cooked by a mistress of the art, topped by a rich pudding . . . !" Yet she also must have wanted more adventure than she could imagine by herself. So she found help. Yeats, Stevens, Eliot, Frost, D. H. Lawrence: she published people who have ceased to be only people for us, because they are preserved in the medium of their poems. This has altered them, and yet she altered them first.

Riding around in one of Chicago's many elevated subway trains, I overhear some of these writers' voices conferring with Monroe and her mutterings in reply to them.

Sherwood Anderson is one of the voices. Though not really at his best in a poem, Anderson wrote some of the most poetically unsettling fiction that one is likely to find, and in a little story, "Milk Bottles," drew a picture of Chicago going oozily bad in summer that still seems true. Regardless of his success with prose, he wanted very much for his poetry to be published by Miss Monroe. Sometimes he wrote to her in quest of this on the letterhead of the company that employed him, Critchfield & Co. Advertising & Merchandising Agents. The letterhead's typography looks rigidly quaint now.

"I just got your note about the luncheon for the Untermeyers," he tells Harriet in April, 1921. "At the time of the luncheon I was in the hospital just having had my tonsils dug out." Half a year later, tonsils forgotten, he confides, referring to a poem he apparently had sent to her, "I am afraid what poetic conception I have is not very clearly related to anything." Despite his seeming humility, Anderson also made a point of dismissing (gently) Monroe's negative comments on his poetry as "not very illuminating."

One of the possibly unappreciated stanzas:

Would that the light of life could come clammering [sic]
through the narrow
closed gates of myself!
Would that the gates could be broken and light come to flood
the dark
interior of me!

The poet and journalist Carl Sandburg, who occasionally filled in as a so-called Emergency Associate Editor at her magazine, admired Monroe's gumption in doing things her way and getting noticed quickly by her readers and writers for a degree of cosmopolitan self-confidence that may have surprised them. "The Julia Cooley review is terrific," he writes her in 1917. "Are you starting a new cult aimed at telling the God's truth, no matter what?" He dispatched notes to Monroe on his *Chicago Daily News* stationery. A long-ago reader's report from Sandburg, the intrepid editor emergent, reads: "I think Madame Sherry has much more to say than most of the published and accepted poets." At the bottom of his affidavit, someone else has penciled, "Well, I don't agree." Harriet's ghost?

Twenty-two-year-old William Saroyan wrote her at touching length in 1931 about his assessment of the state of poetry. His account is intelligent but also inflated with a cub's washy sense of discovery, and whatever poems he sent along to her with it must not have suited the magazine; a spruce note (like the ghostly rejoinder on the Sandburg testimonial) comments: "Retd—prosy." Five weeks later, Saroyan rebounded, confessing to the editor, "I was amused with your honest opinion of the poems I sent you: amused, I mean, with myself for sending them. I agree. I was having fun, not writing poetry." He elaborated, "Occasionally I feel I may ultimately write a good poem, and this is a fine state of affairs: it sort of helps to keep one's identity in good shape. And if I do not write a good poem what does it matter? I will have at least been ready."

With charming ebullience, writers would sometimes submit too many poems all at once to Monroe and her staff. Take the case of Osbert Sitwell, addressing Harriet in 1921.

Dear Miss Harriet Monroe,

I have the pleasure of submitting to you 3 poems by myself and 3 by my brother. We should be so delighted if you should publish them.

I hope I am not overwhelming you with my family?

Other poets were more circumspect. The teensy, drab, inoffensive handwriting in pencil of Wallace Stevens on yellow, ruled paper arrived in a letter he mailed to Chicago from Woodstock, New York, in 1917, and the poems that came with it were also written on yellow, ruled paper in pencil. It's as though Stevens wanted to keep himself secret, like a distant rumor. But his handwriting becomes much easier to read in the poems than in the letter, even when a substantial French epigraph precedes a long sequence of stanzas. His ordinarily difficult hand—sharp, spiky, spigotted—seems to have been tamed or cajoled by the poetry. He confided in 1920, "Dear Miss Monroe: I am much more modest than you think, or than the overblown bloom I am suggests."

*Poetry* magazine is best known for the writers whom Monroe, with her descendants and disciples, has helped to discover, not for the poets whose work has been rejected there over the years. But most poets, of course, never were or will be published in *Poetry*, no matter how much they may wish for it. The pressure of all their unfulfilled longing, decades old, feels present to me, like another sort of haunting.

As if responding to that pressure in her own day, Mrs. Alice Corbin Henderson, one of Harriet's editorial deputies, wrote an editorial in the July 1916 issue of *Poetry* entitled "The Rejection Slip." She herself had sent many such slips on their doleful way. Henderson begins by observing in her editorial that would-be poets outnumber by far the magazine's actual subscribers, then complains that the poets harass *Poetry*'s editors with too much verse—and with the unrealistic expectation that every submission arriving in Chicago will somehow deserve and inspire a detailed letter from the editor, even if (especially if?) the poetry has been declined for publication.

Mrs. Henderson objects to that pesky attitude. Alluding to the abilities of any conscientious editor, she declares in the editorial, "One can not turn oneself into a human machine; the capacity even of an inhuman machine is limited." (I imagine Harriet nodding nearby in moral agreement.) Then Alice notes, "What sort of rejection slip would not be brutal and dispiriting?" It is difficult, even now, to answer her satisfactorily. She defends her magazine's editorial policies and standards: "All the verse that has come into this office up-to-date has been extremely important, and the editors have not been willing to relegate [reading] this to underlings or to outside readers." (As other magazines did and have continued to do.) Finally, as if giving voice to a frustration of rich vintage, she claims, "The rejection slip hurts the editor far more than it does the poet. The poet *knows* that he is a genius; and the editor still hopes to discover that he is in each manuscript examined. The editor has a hundred sorrows for the poet's one."

To me her reasoning seems fatuous; the primary pain of editors is almost sure to lie elsewhere. But for writers, nearly any rejection of their work—and especially the latest in a series—has to cause consternation, whether it takes shape as a rejection slip or as a published book review. As a sometime arts critic for Chicago newspapers, Monroe was more than willing to air her disapproval in the public pages. Decidedly averse to a newspaper review of his work written by Monroe in 1907, the architect Frank Lloyd Wright had his say about the proper uses of criticism in a voluminous letter written to her on his magnificent personal stationery. The letter infuriated her with its somber tirade, inked on lofty, tawny folded sheets that today can be found and unfolded in Monroe's Chicago archive.

> Personally [Wright wrote], I am hungry for the honest, genuine criticism that searches the soul of the thing and sifts its form. Praise isn't needed especially. There is enough of that, such as it is, but we all need intelligent painstaking inquiry leading into the nature of the proposition to be characterized before with airy grace the subject is lightly touched up with House Beautiful [sic] English for the mob.

Monroe's pencil draft of the answer she sent to Wright is fervent, brisk, and piercing, as though little electrified tines were riding on the backs of her consonants. He was so impressed by her pugilism that he later tried to mollify her.

Though equally vivid in temperament, the far more tactful Marianne Moore wrote as a young woman to Monroe in a lusciously balanced hand, rounded and swirling yet upright. Her notepaper in 1915 was gray-green, soft, and durable, a spiritual Japanese fabric drenched in mild aqua. (Years later, when she was living in Brooklyn, her handwriting seems to have lost its flavorful pulse, and she favored plain bond. While still erect, the handwriting thinned—the swing had left it.) Anyhow, the intent and politic Moore, writing to Monroe, left no doubt about her gratitude for any editorial scrap of advice her poems might receive at the time. She was twenty-seven. To Harriet she wrote, "Printed slips are enigmatic things and I thank you for your criticism of my poems. I shall try to profit by it."

# Pleasures of a Critic

READERS TEND TO REGARD CRITICISM as a dreary sidekick of writing, a shadowy, annoying, or foul accomplice to art—a sham authority. How many of us actually expect to take pleasure in critical paragraphs? How many would rather read critic so-and-so than the poet she criticizes? Dismissed as second-string in literature, and miffed because of it, the critic may aim too low, smudge her words—shuffle and equivocate—before the reader. Her prose becomes dull. She apologizes for her insignificance. She bows redundantly to her betters, the poets and the novelists. She pleads haplessly for more time, editorial space, and money from her well-meaning editors, hoping somehow to dignify and extend her intrinsically minor line of work.

A deep conviction of their inconsequentiality probably prevents some critics from making the most of themselves and their genre: they simplify, shorten, get the thing done much too efficiently, or write almost inaudibly, as though they were not really anyone, or were not really writing. Not enough critics rebel; not enough become publishers, for instance, who are better able by the nature of their job to revise conventional or commercial editorial formulas.

Short of rebelling, when they finally come to feel inconsolably doubtful of their role, critics may barricade themselves too exclusively within the guild of journalists, or within the guild of scholars. You can sometimes overhear them muttering the season's fave clichés, even if you are not a guild member: talk streams of a "pellucid" debut novel, which "problematizes" the narrator, or of the "plangency" of a certain ghazal.

Too few reviewers write for the common reader, whoever that is. They have chosen a coterie of friends as ears, or have been forced to serve a dubious "market" with their prose, or have succumbed to the difficult demands of a private muse. When the general reader disappears, part of the pleasure of criticism flees, also.

Despite such stumbling blocks, it's still possible to be a critic and do it well. On my list of indispensable prose books about poetry are recent essay collections by Eliot Weinberger, Alan Shapiro, and Helen Vendler, for example. Yet these exceptions (and others) may help to prove the rule: critics don't have enough readers, and can't write well enough without them.

☒

FOR ME AS A READER, the pleasures of criticism come down to the chance to eavesdrop on somebody who is much smarter than I am—who can think better, with more courage, freedom, clarity, and precision than I can. Unfairly, most contemporary institutions, from university writing programs to arts funders and granting agencies, don't consider criticism to be an imaginative or personal form of writing. But I do.

Critics can change your mind by using theirs. What could be more exhilarating or creative? That criticism is a commentary doesn't necessarily rob it of originary power. Though many critics appear to forfeit this power, so do various poets and novelists. Failure is a part of the game for us all.

When I eavesdropped one winter on a seminar given by Vendler on Shakespeare's sonnets at the 92nd Street Y in New York, the ingenuity of her analysis, wired by her wit, seemed as compelling in its way as the Shakespeare, like another voice harmonizing with his. I would much rather follow both voices than have to choose between them. The subsequent publication of her book, *The Art of Shakespeare's Sonnets* (Harvard University Press, 1997), has prolonged my eavesdropping.

In a different sense, poet Alan Shapiro's *The Last Happy Occasion* (University of Chicago Press, 1996), a gathering of memoiristic essays addressing the changing place of poetry in his life, brought me criticism as a primary voice, not an also-ran. Rather than scrutinizing individual poems, Shapiro contextualizes poetry in literary and personal terms. He suggests or explains what certain poets have meant to him, and why. He keeps on thinking, and because he can, I want to.

The poet, translator, editor, and essayist Eliot Weinberger serves readers, too, as a kind of investigative reporter on poetry. His role is novel, sometimes antagonizing, and typically insightful. Especially when he writes about the politics of the poetry world—cultural and personal infighting among writers, schools of thought, or institutions—Weinberger braves backlash with his candor and an uncompromising perspective. He questions and judges; some would prefer he didn't. Weinberger's recent book, *Written Reaction* (Marsilio Publishers, 1996), offers criticism not only of poets or poems but of the society that receives, thwarts, and helps to invent them.

Still, when I think "critic" and "poetry," I think of the poet and critic Randall Jarrell (1914–1965), who presided over another American literary era with an exuberance that is unusual no matter how you measure it. I have been reading and rereading him for months, taken aback by what's before me.

At first I suspected that Jarrell's brilliance as a poetry critic was partly a matter of temperament, like a dapper, devil-may-care toaster that sometimes overheats pugnaciously. And so I wanted to know what he had been like as a person; he seems like such an intriguing maverick. Now, though, I believe his brilliance was largely a matter (besides talent) of pleasure found and relished. Jarrell took more than his share of pleasure from poetry, and even from poetry criticism. The pleasure he took seemed to border on hot-rod hedonism.

A sign of the hedonist maverick in him: although from 1935 to 1964 he wrote about Yvor Winters, W. H. Auden, Kenneth Patchen, Muriel Rukeyser, Elizabeth Bishop, Ezra Pound, Allen Tate, Willa Cather, Franz Kafka, T. S. Eliot, e. e. cummings, Robert Lowell, André Malraux, Marianne Moore, R. S. Crane, Rudyard Kipling, Adrienne Rich, and others, Jarrell also wrote about fast cars and Ernie Pyle, the World War II correspondent. His appetite for pleasure, earthily aesthetic, is unmistakable in "The Little Cars," a piece about auto racing written in 1954. It begins like this:

> Someday, driving along the highway, you will see the
> traffic begin to change. Among the lanes of ordinary
> cars, streaming by like big, sedate, efficient hens, two or
> three little dyed Easter chicks of cars will appear—then
> half a dozen, dozens, hundreds. The exhausts of the
> small engines make a sharp, bright, crackling sound (if

you lean closer you will hear their owners saying, "Listen to that exhaust!") or else a little bubbling roar, the sound a child makes playing with a bubble pipe. . . . A few of the cars have a sleek, nasty look, as if they wanted to go a hundred and fifty and despised traffic, but the rest have a gay, light, irresponsible air—they are perfect meringues of cars. They seem all for fun and hardly at all for transportation; the ordinary automobiles alongside look like a vocation with a pension at the end, and the little ones like a vacation.

In describing the vim of the vehicle, Jarrell also suggests his vim as a writer. The pleasure given by the cars is readily, happily recognized and registered, because Jarrell can respond with a similar stylishness. Conspicuous in the writing is the joystick of Jarrell's wit, used not only to qualify or punctuate the comments but also to form thought and complete it. His voice falls naturally into a speedy lyric patter, which is his answer to mechanical grace. As the auto critic, he isn't only watching, he is writing—he is doing. Doing no less than a car does.

But pleasure is easy to find in fast cars and, one might suppose, less easily had in poems. Isn't car criticism a fairly carefree assignment, after all, with the fun foreordained? Surely Jarrell as critic must be on holiday here from his real job of book reviewing for the *Nation*, the *New Republic*, and the *American Scholar*.

Perhaps, but Jarrell was very much in earnest about his pleasure, wherever he could find it. And he found it in unlikely places—in the worst of cars and in the least of poems.

Jarrell's imagination sometimes seems to have engaged more fully and raptly with bad news than with good, regardless of his subject's particulars. He was a critic; he depended on the negative to keep him going. He wasn't afraid of it—the negative delighted and honed him. And so in closing his auto essay he lights with sureness of finale on the topic of egregious drivers and vehicles, giving them a delicious send-off. His metaphors playfully compete with the absurdity that he describes, and then they win.

> Most works of art are, necessarily, bad, and so are most races; one suffers through the many for the few. Ladies' races, on the West Coast, are Sleeping Beauty affairs won by Josie von Neumann, her long black hair streaming in the wind; 500 c.c. cars are abject skeletal objects that could skitter under your dining-room table, and one of their races is like a Marathon of water spiders. Motor-cycle races—forty copies of Superman going by with a terrible sound, hunched over their handle bars like tailors on magic bicycles—are rarest of all, but worst of all; worse even than stock Jaguar races, where every turn is torture, the brakes are always screaming, and the inside rear wheel is always just about to lift. The ideally awful race, I think, would be between ladies, stock Jaguars, 500 c.c. cars, motorcycles, and Edith Sitwell.

Another pleasure for me in the car criticism is Jarrell's tendency to imply a story, in lyric snatches, rather than just criticize: Josie's streaming black hair establishes her as a fleeting but fascinating character, and the motorcyclists are a vivid fairy-tale corps. Jarrell's imaginary "awful race" takes the page vigorously, like a cartoon that can never be purged. This is criticism as a conjuring act.

Jarrell made his name early by writing negative reviews of

poetry. The very brief ones can now seem show-offy, their dismissive judgments hurled with a fierce zeal. In 1948, he dealt with *The Kid,* a book of poems by Conrad Aiken, in a single paragraph.

> Conrad Aiken's *The Kid* is one of those manufactured, sponsored, "American" epics: a surprisingly crude hodgepodge of store-bought homespun, of Madison Square Garden patriotism, of Johnny Appleseed and Moby Dick and Paul Revere and the Grand Canyon, all banged out in conscientiously rough rhymes, meter, and grammar—"just like a ballad." There is something a little too musically ectoplasmic, too pretty-pretty, about Mr. Aiken's best poems; but one longs for them as one wanders, like an imported camel, through the Great American Desert of *The Kid.*

Seven years earlier, Jarrell had written of Aiken's *And in the Human Heart*:

> The content of Mr. Aiken's best poems has almost disappeared; these are only their emptied and enormously inflated rhetorical shells.

What kind of anger could motivate the trashing of a writer who was one of the poet Jarrell's peers?

Jarrell's was a personal, moral, and literary anger. He published a satirical novel, *Pictures from an Institution,* in 1954; he respected malice as a technique of literature, and anger naturally became part of his critical voice. The voice also included lyric tenderness, but anger helped to make his voice really unusual and really his, because the anger was allowed, not suppressed. For him anger was a pleasure, and for me it is that, some of the time.

If the source of the anger lay in his nature, it also grew out of the social, political, and economic facts of poetry writing, reading, publishing, and criticism, facts that Jarrell laid out with particular sparkle, amusement, and irritation in two essays, "Contemporary Poetry Criticism" (1941) and "Poets, Critics, and Readers" (1954). The first piece shows his pragmatic understanding of criticism's purpose in a commercial world.

> From the publisher's point of view criticism is a quite important subspecies of advertising; reviews are free publicity, free testimonials.... Editors seldom print unfavorable articles on poets, so critics rarely write them.... Good criticism, which points out badness or mediocrity, and actually scares away buyers from most books, is something the publishers necessarily cannot tolerate.

Given these circumstances, true now as then, how could a critic of Jarrell's tenacious intensity get his work written, published, and read? Perhaps only in a state of periodic righteous pique—by force of his outraged resistance. Like his fellow critics, he could write for literary magazines and a few enlightened others. But to be a critic was to war with the publishing establishment. Jarrell must have enjoyed the warring, even if it tired him out.

His essay "Poets, Critics, and Readers" is an equally accurate but more complex and bemusing meditation on the vanishing of poetry readers and the inability of critics to make up for their loss. "Art is long and critics are the insects of the day," declared Jarrell harshly, perhaps weary of his war, perhaps regretting the time he had poured into criticism at the expense of his poetry. While he admits that the very best critics may harbor a literary promise similar to that of poets and novelists, he doesn't believe that many are apt to make good on it. Most wouldn't even realize that it was possible. His picture is gloomy, colored with futility in every corner.

Despite this, the essay reveals Jarrell as the rare critic who can dispute with himself over his own worth in public, demanding more of his criticism than anyone else would. Criticism was a cathartic adventure for him, and what it was for him, it could yet be for us.

# The Slant of the Sidelong:
# Partiality and a Poet

WHAT DOES IT MEAN TO BE PARTIAL? To see or experience less than the total. To favor a view that is singular, bearing down with insistence on an aspect of experience in hopes of illuminating it.

To some extent, partiality is inborn in an observer; to some extent, it is chosen by her. When indulged, it leads to restriction, dislocation, and distortion. But when exercised with intelligence and daring, partiality will magnify the objects of perception and undertake a rare understanding. Partiality can bring extraordinary power not only to a "partial" observer, but to an audience or a community.

All poets, like all people, are partial in one way or another, yet some cultivate their partiality, study it, or bow to it with such devotion that partiality itself becomes a kind of art, a sort of hubris, a heroism, or a creed of service. Emily Dickinson is an exemplar of such an extreme position. Her poetry often either seizes partiality as a theme or demonstrates the work and play of a "partial" mind with delight. Her point of view is emphatically partial and paradoxically forceful; the power of her perception is singular, not narrow. For that reason, to write critically about her "partial" view may help to characterize her originality as a poet.

The symptoms of her partiality include an abstemious concision of form, a suspenseful asperity of tone, and an indirection of approach to subject; a covert but furiously intent will to see and to report; and a willingness to receive sensation or knowledge as a beneficent scourge. The act of seeing, and the imposition of imaginative judgment, are inherently impertinent. For these acts call Dickinson's spiritual rank into question. Though a servant of God, she continually asserts her right to know more, at times with misgivings, yet with marked appetite. That is one reason for the propulsive drama of her poems. They are not only about seeing. Instead, they are about mortal might and the imperative need to rebel from it for something mightier.

So many of the poems comment on perception that it seems difficult to limit discussion to a few. Dickinson's poems about partiality fall into various categories (some belong to more than one, and others to no category). There are those that consider partiality with metaphors involving light and darkness; others that consider it in terms of space, scale, scope, reduction, and means of measurement. Still others summon up a vision of remarkable things seen, and the objects themselves help to expose the act of being seen partially. Others muse on the need to speak or to write, or on a contrary need to desist, introducing a tension into art. And a few broach partiality somewhat more directly.

Poem 258, which begins "There's a certain Slant of light," offers an example of the last type.

There's a certain Slant of light,
Winter Afternoons—
That oppresses, like the Heft
Of Cathedral Tunes—

Heavenly Hurt, it gives us—
We can find no scar,
But internal difference,
Where the Meanings, are—

None may teach it—Any—
'Tis the Seal Despair—
An imperial affliction
Sent us of the Air—

When it comes, the Landscape listens—
Shadows—hold their breath—
When it goes, 'tis like the Distance
On the look of Death—

In the poem, the "Slant" of light can be understood as representing and recommending a singular perspective, not named or credited, perceived by an anonymous multitude ("us") at cost to their short-term comfort. "Slant" suggests a remote origin, a point of view beyond the general or ordinary, a finite path chosen by an infinite intelligence capable of penetrating to the deepest point of any object or receiver. Slant concentrates light as if with purpose, isolating itself from a larger context. Slant also suggests direction, a direction that is boldly sidelong and dissenting. Yet the poem doesn't specify an origin or a direction for the slant of light, only a singularity of position. (The poet, like the multitudes, seems able only to receive the light, to witness it.) Power emanates from that singularity, but can't be anticipated or concluded. The authority of the slant is dreadful.

The poem concerns authority as much as it does light or vision. For the slant of light "oppresses" with a somber weight, inflicting hurt with an "imperial" disdain for clarity. The authority of the slant is so egregiously commanding that it threatens the survival of anyone or anything receiving it. Then what redeems the slant or makes it valuable?

The strength of the slant is furtive, indirect, and unexpected in its course. Witnesses will have to search it out by marshaling a comparable ingenuity of indirection. However, in the poem this sort of action isn't forecast or performed. Dickinson seems too busy observing and weighing the action of the slant to undertake one of her own.

## Partiality and a Reader

SOMETIMES DIFFICULTY SEEMS TO BE the great cause of criticism. If a poem is not "difficult" enough, then a theoretical perspective or an individual predilection can make it so, recruiting and redeeming the poem for the purposes of criticism, and requiring extensive investigation and interpretation. I am disputatious, curious, and resistant, and so I have no objection to difficulty if it is genuine. But I think difficulty can't be solved, and perhaps shouldn't be; it can only be approached, and is probably best approached indirectly. It is subject to view, and not subject to remedy. Real difficulty may not lend itself to a frontal dissection, because real difficulty did not arise frontally; its development was partially concealed or roundabout. So a critic had better adapt to this fact, and respect it: one cannot "finish knowing" a poem, especially if the poem itself knows very much. And one form of adaptation to difficulty of this sort is the series of glimpses as a favored and partial mode of looking and knowing.

Some of Dickinson's poems invite these glimpses. The poems that do aren't necessarily her surpassing achievements. Yet the poems pose an interpretive challenge by refusing to pose any, by resisting the very prospect, by retreating from the onset of light or a gaze. Unusually cryptic and self-contained, these poems seem to be the products of extraction, violence, a rivening. The critical glimpse or series of glimpses must fall on the poems without grand ambition to disassemble them; they'd refuse it. Instead, a glimpse sneaks in, brushes against hard boundaries, seeking contact and impressions; then withdraws; then seeks the boundaries again. It is an impulsive but considered way of looking at a poem that owns its own impulses stealthily.

Consider poem 1261, which begins "A Word dropped careless on a Page."

A Word dropped careless on a Page
May stimulate an eye
When folded in perpetual seam
The Wrinkled Maker lie

Infection in the sentence breeds
We may inhale Despair
At distances of Centuries
From the Malaria —

A series of glimpses might return from the poem with these fleeting, sometimes contradictory inferences and reports:

1. The seam protects the venerably wrinkled Maker, or poet, from the Word that he has made—and fortunately so, since the Word is dangerous.

2. The Maker of the Word (the poet) only supposes that he made it. Sealed off in helpless sanctity, like a wrinkled, unborn infant, he can create little besides wrinkles, while the "careless" Word descends with arrogant cheer to the Page from another, more formidable Maker.

3. Original creation is not possible for people. Only a god can create; secondary makers, or poets, can witness creation but must protect themselves from its power, which could destroy them. They are too easily seduced by it, and aren't capable of resisting.

4. Poets may envy a god and his capacity for creation, or despair that they cannot create like him. Even so, envy and despair do not improve their lot. The poet's awareness of his "sentence" as a helplessly secondary also-ran in matters of creation only emphasizes the "distances" separating him from divine power and virus. And so he pines, infected.

5. The power of a Word is most redoubtable when the Maker is absent, unable to take credit, unable to be interviewed, supplanted by the very Word.

6. The perfect Word banishes its maker, causes him to sicken or perish of "infection" bred by the Word's absolute dominion. The Word renders the writer irrelevant, even turns against him.

7. Mortal illness, which confronts the ill with the fact of mortality, is a difficult blessing, but still a blessing. If words can persuade us of mortality in a sort of illness or infection, then they deserve their dominion.

8. Creation offers a death to the creator, and endangers bystanders, too. Every poem written in this spirit is an act of desperate heroism.

9. The stimulated eye, in reading this poem, is the beneficiary of the poem, not only because the eye is stimulated by reading, but also because the eye is challenged to undertake an angle of vision, to subscribe to a partiality, to a way of seeing.

10. The passive or absent Maker, and the propitious yet "careless," unasserting Word, have no means of proposing or engaging with such an angle of vision. Only the stimulated eye, left free, can loom over a scene of despair and sickness, and survive them.

11. The all-powerful eye must decide on its own angle. Dickinson won't recommend one.

12. The eye is only an eye, independent of human motive. Social relations don't determine perception, or even stimulate it. Perception is a nonnegotiable act in which other readers, and certainly all creators, are forgotten. The eye is disassociated and supreme.

13. The eye is supreme, and it is solitary, irreversibly isolated in exaltation. No more extreme demand could be made of it than to see—to see partially.

Is it necessary to choose from among these interpretive possibilities? Yes, eventually; a partial reader will. But it may be wiser to encounter difficulty in a poem by seeking out "possibilities" as the best adventure in a series of glimpses that meet the poem. Partiality should offer this sort of interpretive license.

## Where Partiality Begins: A Few Scenes

TO BEGIN TO "KNOW" A POEM assumes a habit of knowing formed, by chance, in living. And so it seems reasonable to pause and offer a sidelong glance at the world just beyond Dickinson, and even beyond poetry, in search of a "slant" in the mind of a reader who hopes to give Dickinson a home in consciousness.

Of course, I am that reader, engaged like everyone else in the daily work of self-justification. Naturally, I am "partial": I believe in what I see, or I reject it, but I shape it continually. I am my own authority.

Yet I am also looking, like many, to be shaped. The lifelong business of striking a balance between seeing what one can and seeking what one wants is not just a solitary labor. It also presents a rich opportunity for intercession from abroad.

Intercession disputes the security of one's position, whatever that was. A foreign authority who disputes yours challenges your partiality, expanding your scope, preventing too much stability, creed-mongering, and the institutionalization of the self. Incoming details and information can distract, helpfully; their "slant" tutors, with words or without.

Nature, for instance, once a teacher of Dickinson, still teaches us. Nature intercedes with us. In closing, then, a few more glimpses of the partial and arguments in favor of it.

# A Bird on a Branch

THE SEASON IS FALL, and animals are preparing for change, whether this means bolting from the continent or retiring underground. In the midst of the massive, fragmentary dash, I happen to pause and catch sight of a bird, who is also pausing.

My view of him is odd, intimate, discrepant. Perhaps he feels careless because he knows he will leave this place soon, possibly forever. Not even a foot away, he perches recklessly on a branch, slightly above me, head tilted high, not bothering to watch me watching him. The angle of vision he offers means I can see under him on the way up to his beak, which is the topmost point. I feel privileged to see the bird's underside — startlingly, the underside is fastidiously tailored and bright yellow, though the bird isn't yellow otherwise. I have never glimpsed this before, and his yellow seems to reward the wayward, unexpected glance.

But the glance lasts only for an instant before he flies off. And I suspected that it would be brief. Knowing this, I forsook a more systematic look to peer mainly at one small place. And I decided I had seen what mattered most about the bird. I concluded that I hadn't seen any other bird adequately before. This view was the first to surprise me, to lunge from the ordinary into a perception of strangeness. I believed that I had seen not just a bird but a piece of elation, like a flame before it settles and dies.

# The Farm in the Fence

MOST VISITORS OF FARMS WANT TO SEE HERDS. And they can; nearly all farms have them. But I believe I've seen more through the measly gaps in a fence than when evening feeding brought heifer upon heifer bounding into full sight all at once.

Still, I was taken aback to realize this. I was sitting near a field in the sun and flirting by eye with the gaps between the rails of a fence, playing with the shapes of interrupted space, and might have done no more if a goat hadn't ambled into view behind the fence in the field. I could only see a small fragment of goat at a time, which another observer might have found annoying. I didn't, because in this way I was able to appreciate the goat as if before its creation had been completed. That seemed fortunate.

I studied parts: eye, angular in shape, not rounded; like an insect's, but with more sense of dwelling within the eye. Ears, of no esprit; they flopped, as no other part of the goat did—very odd. Muzzle, wearing a constant mild smile, utterly counter to goat stereotype; a muzzle to trust, despite the reputation for scandalous grazing. And so on. The details roused the mind and confronted clichés kept there, with a hooved kick, playful. The goat continued moving, and I continued looking, until the animal's image had acquired a generic clarity and a familial warmth, framed like a photograph jostled in a locket. The implicit challenge of the partial sight was one I chose to neglect: that of putting the goat back together again, having glimpsed so many transits and particulars. I enjoyed the parts far too much to forfeit the pleasure of my glimpses by merging these into a false, convenient compendium.

# The Impossible Vista

AFTER A LONG WALK ON THE BEACH spent inspecting small things (rocks, hermit crabs, snippets of seaweed), I retreated to a dune for a respite and found, to my chagrin, a sweeping vista visible from the sandy peak. A large marsh extended, with woods in back. I looked, uncertain of where to look, while winds tossed the reeds in seeming sequence and ducks followed apparent paths in the pond waters.

A beautiful sight, and my eyes lingered, but I could do little with what I saw. It was too general, and my inclusive, overlooking perspective did not make seeing easy; quite the contrary. If I sought out a detail (a frond, a bill), it was nearly buried in the whole, and half unwilling to emerge. Besides, in seizing one detail, or trying to, I found that others competed with it for my attention. So much of what I saw was in motion that the moments overtook one another before I could catch up with them.

I was looking at a habitat that I couldn't inhabit, at least not with partiality as my guide. And I soon looked away. A tiny spider flung himself at my face from a nearby bush, swinging along a transparent line. I looked him up and down (he was very like a gorilla in miniature) and felt I had found my place again. I turned my back on vista.

The best observers, maybe, must be partial; they turn an inward eye outward.

# THE AUTHOR

Evelyn Aikman

MOLLY McQUADE's essays and criticism have appeared in *The Village Voice, Hungry Mind Review, New England Review, Boston Review, Newsday,* the *Chicago Tribune,* and elsewhere. She has served as editor of the monthly *Poetry Calendar* magazine, and previously founded and edited the poetry review column of *Publishers Weekly.* Her writing has received fellowships and awards from the New York Foundation for the Arts, the Pew Charitable Trusts, the National Council of Teachers of English, and the Illinois Arts Council. Her first book, *An Unsentimental Education,* a collection of biographical portraits of writers, was published in 1995 by the University of Chicago Press. Her poetry, nominated twice for a Pushcart Prize, has appeared or is forthcoming in *North American Review, Pequod, The Paris Review,* and *Western Humanities Review.* A contributing editor for *Kirkus Reviews* and for the Graywolf Press, as well as a columnist for *Booklist,* she has also been a board member of the National Book Critics Circle.